SOUVENIR OF DAYTONIA.

Marula

An imprint of Arcadia Publishing

Souvenir of Daytonia
by the Daytonia Souvenir Committee

A Marula Historical Reprint
Originally published in 1896

Published by Arcadia Publishing
Charleston SC

ISBN 978-0-7385-9486-6

Printed in the United States of America

For all general information contact Arcadia Publishing at:
Telephone 843-853-2070
Fax 843-853-0044
E-mail sales@arcadiapublishing.com
For customer service and orders:
Toll-Free 1-888-313-2665

Visit us on the Internet at www.arcadiapublishing.com

SOUVENIR OF DAYTONIA

PREFACE.

HARRY WEIDNER.

THE production of DAYTONIA, spectacular in scenery and historical in portrayal, given by the Ladies and Gentlemen of Dayton, aims to serve two commendable purposes.

First, as a continued commemoration of Dayton's Centennial Anniversary, which was begun with an ardor and appropriateness commensurate with the importance of the gala event.

Daytonians hold in profound reverence the memories of their forefathers, who risked their lives and their fortunes in subduing the unbroken forest and its savage denizens, and in laying strong, wide, and deep the foundations of a city which to-day contains as many elements of advancement, and is endowed with as many of the attributes of genuine happiness, as any city in the United States.

There is a just cause for congratulation in the growth and development of Dayton. Its magnificence is a crowning monument to the enlightenment and progressiveness of its citizens—a devout, law-abiding, and upright people, whose stalwart and robust Americanism constitutes their chief excellence. It is no such Americanism as turns up its pantaloons every time it rains in London, or affects a pronunciation of our glorious tongue unknown to lexicons, but presumed to be an echo of the British Isles. Far from it. Dayton proudly boasts of an exalted citizenship, imbued with the spirit of an undying loyalty to country, whose pride and inspiration are not in Frederick the Great, or Louis XIV., or William the Conqueror; not in a hero of England, or of Germany, or of France, or of Ireland, but in George Washington and Abraham Lincoln.

Dayton, too, is happily situated, nestling in the lap of a teeming valley. It appears like a beautiful solitaire in the golden luxuriance of its picturesque environments, presenting a spectacle of surpassing beauty, calm as the vale of Avoca, fair as the famous Æsopus, and peaceful as the valley of Tempe. The gentle Miami, in its sinuous flow, laves the city's feet, as it wends its downward way. Though it bears not on its placid bosom the commerce of a great people, yet, in its tranquillity, it is dearer to us than the blue Danube, with all its poetry, or the Rhine, with all its legends. Verily, where is a spot approaching nearer the fabled garden of the Hesperides, with all its imagined splendors, than the Gem City of the Miami Valley, where Venus herself might enjoy the charms and loveliness of her daughters?

Aside from its commemorative feature, the production of DAYTONIA is for the benefit of the St. Elizabeth and Deaconess Hospitals. Both institutions are an enduring honor to our magnificent, thrifty, and far-famed Gem City, to which she can point with the same pride which Cornelia manifested in her children. And who can speak in amply panegyrical terms of that noble band of nurses, the sweet sisters and good deaconesses, the comforting and ministering angels of the sick-room, where the opportunities for their usefulness are as illimitable as the complex ills which flesh is heir to? Their heroic services and indescribable sacrifices are worthy of the highest encomiums. To the friendless sufferers, with no kindly voice to whisper comfort in their sorrows; no hand to soften the asperities with which this world's conflict will harden the downiest pillow; no kindred heart in whose sympathetic throbbings they can read the alphabet of love, how blest their voices, that, like genial showers poured on the desert, gladden as they flow, and cheer the sinking heart; how matchless their fidelity, inviolable as the covenant of the Most High, their purity unsullied as the light of heaven!

In conclusion, the Executive Committee, through the Souvenir Committee, desires to express its deepest gratitude:

First, to Director-General Harry E. Feicht, whose unflagging zeal and unselfish devotion have done so much to further this laudable enterprise. His intense interest in its successful culmination touched the extremest limit of exultant enthusiasm, constantly inspiring others to renewed endeavor.

Second, to the Press, so kindly, generous, and patriotic in its spirit and so powerful in its commanding influence, which has made possible the success of DAYTONIA.

Third, to the performers, including all participants in this production, for their painstaking efforts; the beneficent merchants and manufacturers for their spontaneity and liberality both as regards donations and advertisements, and the purchasers of tickets for their manifest interest and loyal support. Few cities in the world can boast of a populace so charitably and public-spiritedly inclined.

Lastly, to all, rich and poor alike, who contributed in the minutest degree to the success of this noble undertaking, either artistically or financially.

SOUVENIR COMMITTEE.

MR. ALFRED A. THRESHER.	MRS. J. B. THRESHER.
MR. HARRY WEIDNER.	MRS. C. E. CORPE.
MR. R. P. BURKHARDT.	MRS. C. J. FERNEDING.
MR. B. F. HARGRAVE.	MRS. P. J. ROTTERMANN.

MISS REBEKAH STRICKLE.

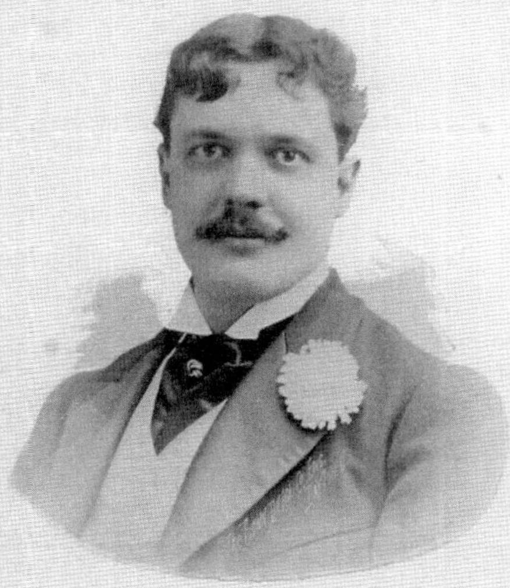

DIRECTOR-GENERAL HARRY E. FEICHT.

HARRY ELLSWORTH FEICHT, whose likeness appears above, the originator of DAYTONIA, a production given under his personal direction, is a Daytonian by birth and education. He is a shining specimen of assiduity and perseverance — eager to do, tireless in energy, persistent in purpose. By his philanthropic and patriotic services — for he is continually promoting some praiseworthy work of public benefaction — he has won the immeasurable admiration and abiding attachment of all true Daytonians.

Harry, as he is familiarly called, is a superb leader, of vigorous intellect, of fertility of resource, and of freshness and originality of genius. He is the very incarnation of honor and probity. Beneath his sunny, ardent, and magnanimous nature there lie a potency of will that knows no impediment and powers of intellectual labor that defy fatigue.

It was he who originated the Charity Circus, so unique in conception. The project was prodigious, and its success proportionate with its immensity. The goodly proceeds replenished, in a measure, the depleted coffers of the St. Elizabeth and Deaconess Hospitals. No more need be said in praise of its projector, though the grandest and most glittering gems of eulogy should be set, diadem-like, on the forefront of flattering language.

Mr. Feicht adds luster to everything he touches, as the sprightly edition of the *Dayton Daily Globe*, bearing date of April 1, 1946, glowingly attests. He also inaugurated the Noise Committee that brought out thirty thousand people at midnight on March 31 to usher in our Centennial year.

ODE TO DAYTON.

MRS. J. B. THRESHER.

ALL hail, thou gem in fairest setting
Of golden fields and emerald hills,
With fringe of woods thy borders fretting,
And gleam of silver on thy rills!

All loyalty to thee forever,
Loved city of our hearts and homes;
Thy children will forget thee never,
No matter where the wanderer roams.

All down the years a light is falling,
The dauntless spirit of the past,
And future days to us are calling
To keep their hope and promise fast.

For men have ventured, hoped, and striven,
To build the Dayton of to-day;
A legacy to us have given
Of effort on a toilsome way.

Oh, may we have by Heaven's blessing
Health, knowledge, cleanliness, and peace,
With love to all our hearts possessing,
While arts and industries increase.

Shine on, then, with increasing glory,
Fair gem, shine on the ages through,
And to those ages tell the story
Of honest sons and daughters true.

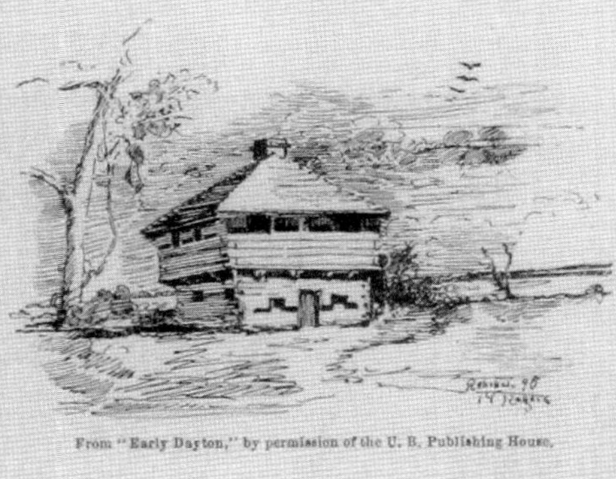

From "Early Dayton," by permission of the U. B. Publishing House.

Stylish Dressers

Should wear the best. You can get it only in the

STEIN BLOCK MAKE AT

The Manhattan
DAYTON, O.

Finest FOOTWEAR in the City. CLOTHES AND SHOES.

JOHN STENGEL & CO.,

MANUFACTURERS OF

FURNITURE.

OFFICE AND FACTORY, 329 and 339 TAYLOR STREET, DAYTON, OHIO.

Attention, Daytonians!

Do not forget the acknowledged fact that

R. W. Koellsch

Sells the Very Best Grades of HARD and SOFT **COAL.**

635 EAST THIRD STREET.

TELEPHONE 972.

GIELE & PFLAUM,

44 East Second Street,

Printers.

Prompt Service.

Telephone 170.

The Monarch Cutter

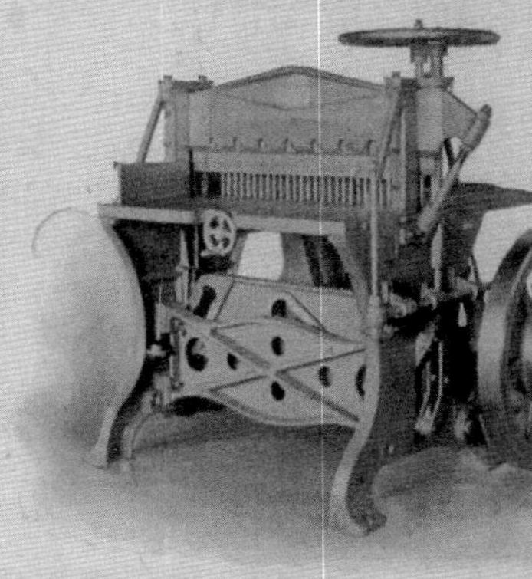

Is revolutionizing the quick, accurate cutting of all paper materials in large quantities.

THE SEYBOLD MACHINE CO.,

Makers of Machinery for Bookbinders, Printers, Lithographers, Paper Mills, Etc.

CHARLES SEYBOLD, Pres. L. W. GUNCKEL, Treas.
B. B. THRESHER, Sec'y.

DAYTON, OHIO, 74 Louie St.

NEW YORK CITY, 44 Centre St. CHICAGO, ILL., 371-373 Dearborn St. ST. LOUIS, MO., 406 N. Third St.

LONDON, E. C., ENGLAND,
No. 2 White Horse Alley, Cowcross St.

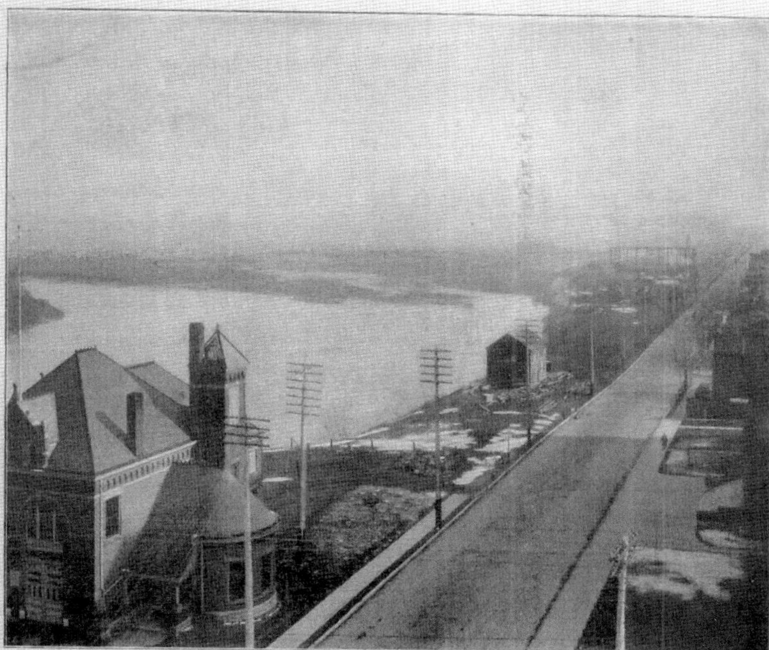

Main Street Hose House. Miami River. Newcom's Tavern. Landing-Place.

From "Early Dayton," by permission of the U. B. Publishing House.

THE LANDING-PLACE AND NEWCOM'S TAVERN IN 1896.

THE breaking waves did not dash high when the little band of pilgrims moored their bark on the banks of the Miami, but in the sunshiny days of early spring on that 1st day of April, one hundred years ago, the flowers and the foliage of the trees were just beginning to unfold, and light snows lay amid the grass, fresh with the greenness of spring. The Miami in 1796 wound through an uninhabited wilderness.

SMOKE

DAYTONIA for a Nickel,

AND

Teutonia Bouquet for a 10-cent Cigar.

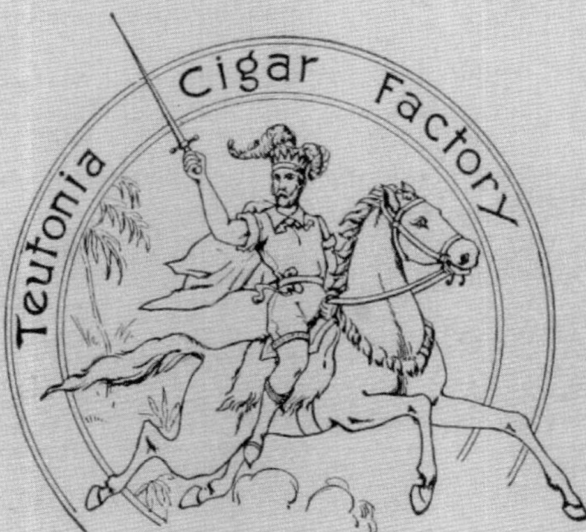

DAYTONIA'S filler is raised only in the Miami Valley, and years of experience have taught us to combine the different grades of tobaccos to make such a quality, equal to the imported Havana tobacco. The wrapper is imported from the island of Sumatra. Give the Daytonia a trial, and you will be surprised what tobacco the Miami Valley produces.

TEUTONIA BOUQUET is our high grade Seed and Havana Cigar. This brand has been before the Dayton public for the last two years, and whoever has smoked them will agree with us that it is the best 10-cent cigar in the market.

H. C. MAHRT CO.

ABORIGINAL DAYTONIANS.

AUGUST F. FOERSTE.

DURING the earlier part of the eighteenth century southwestern Ohio was inhabited by the Miamis. Their permanent villages were located along two main trails, one considerably west of the Great Miami, the other following the Little Miami. The intermediate region, the valley of the Great Miami, was used only as a hunting-ground. The Shawnees, who had emigrated from Florida and Georgia, had settlements on the lower Scioto. Becoming restless, they pushed northward, and in 1740 spread over the area between Springfield and Piqua, formerly occupied by the Miamis. During the French and Indian wars the Miamis sided with the French and the Shawnees with the English. After the defeat of the French, in 1763, the Miamis retreated to Fort Wayne, leaving their territory to the Shawnees.

During the Revolutionary War the Shawnees continued to side with the English, and harassed the settlements in Kentucky until defeated by expeditions from that State in 1786. It was not, however, until Wayne's victory in 1794 that the Shawnees were rendered harmless, and the country was open to settlement. Although the Indians never occupied permanent villages near Dayton, the junction of the Mad and Miami rivers was a favorite camping-ground for their war parties, and burial graves are not uncommon east of Steele's dam. Here the squaws left in charge of the camp may have occasionally raised their favorite corn, beans, pumpkins, and tobacco.

If the mound-builders were distinct from the Indians, they had a curiously similar history. One tribe inhabited the Miami region, and built irregular forts. The nearest of these, including half of Calvary Cemetery, crowns the bluffs, and overlooks the river one hundred and sixty feet below. From this point could be seen the smoke arising from the great Miamisburg mound, seventy feet high, used as a signal station. A second tribe of mound-builders inhabited the Scioto Valley. They were more civilized, and built geometrical earthworks of large proportions in the valleys. They seem at one time to have invaded the valley of the Great Miami, and begun one of their great earthworks five miles south of Dayton, north of Alexandersville. Several circles can still be traced, and a large square was nearly completed, but a portion, now in the woods, was not even begun. The Scioto tribe were probably driven out before they could complete their great earthwork, but it is still a monument to their engineering ability.

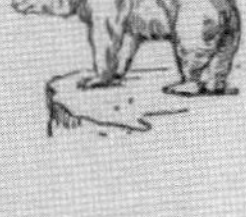

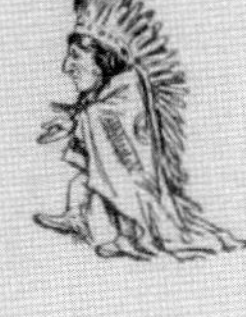

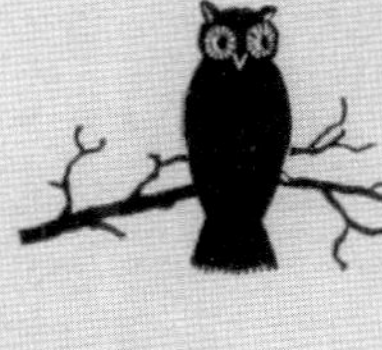

W. P. CALLAHAN. THOS. DE ARMON. W. K. CALLAHAN.

W. P. CALLAHAN & CO.,

FOUNDERS AND MACHINISTS.

MANUFACTURERS OF

Ice and Refrigerating Machinery,

Hydraulic Oil Machinery, Steam Engines, and Cotton Compresses.

DAYTON, OHIO.

Paper Trimming Knives!

Planing Machine Knives.
Various Kinds of Pattern Knives.
Engine Bars and Plates for Paper Mills.

A. A. Simonds & Son, Dayton, O.

Do You Wish the Best Results?

USE

THRESHER'S HIGH GRADE VARNISHES

AND GENUINE KETTLE-BOILED **Linseed Oil**

MADE BY

THRESHER & CO., VARNISH MAKERS, DAYTON, O.

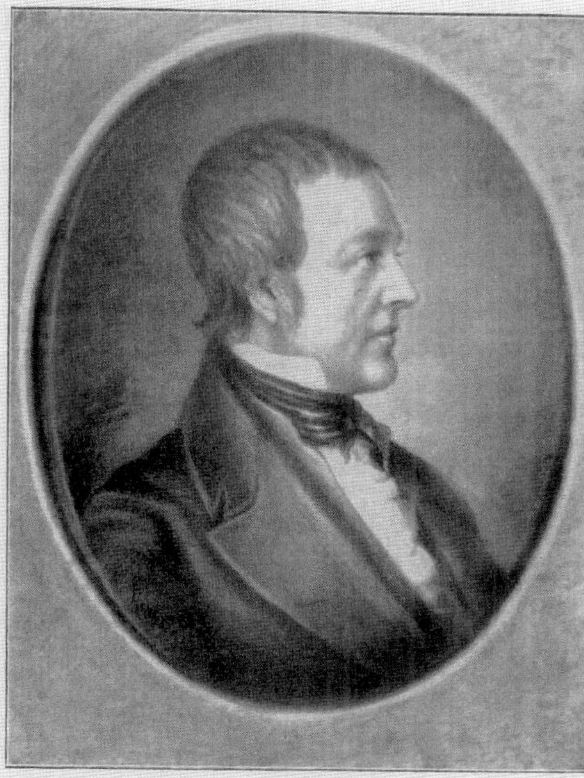

From "Early Dayton," by permission of the U. B. Publishing House.

COLONEL ROBERT PATTERSON

WAS born in 1753 in Bedford County, Pa. In 1786 Patrick Henry, Governor of Virginia, commissioned Robert Patterson a colonel in the "State Line." In 1786 his regiment of Colonel Logan's division marched to destroy the Indian towns on Mad River. But for these battles and victories over the Indians in which Colonel Patterson was for many years engaged, the Dayton settlement would have been an impossibility. His part in the history of our city is of the greatest importance, for he helped win its site from the Indians, and secured a peaceful and prosperous home for the pioneers.

All his later years he was a sufferer from wounds received in his campaigns.

DIERS & TANNER,

Fine Shoes,

104 South Main Street,
DAYTON, OHIO. Davies Building.

E. R. LATIN,

The Hatter and Furnisher,

142 South Main Street,
DAYTON, OHIO. Corner Fifth Street.

Centennial Blend
is the best Coffee ever sold at 22 cents;
Pioneer Blend
is a good one at 25 cents.

THOMSON'S CASH GROCERY.

DEWEESE & BIDLEMAN,

Carpets, Curtains, Mattings,

DRESS GOODS, ETC.

8 East Third Street.

After you see DAYTONIA then go and see

SMITH BROS. & CO.,

IMPORTERS AND DEALERS IN

FINE CHINA AND GLASSWARE.

The only exclusive house in this line in the city.

28 North Main Street. Telephone 849

Gem City Cigar Co.,

JOSEPH J. BUCHER, Prop.

406 South Wayne Ave.

Spring Styles.

CHARCH & WELLS,

TAILORS.

Don't forget to visit

The Boston 99c. Store
for Novelties of all Kinds.

110 East Third Street, DAYTON, OHIO.

LEE WOLF & BRO.,

BOOKS,

Stationery.

Telephone 440.

BURKHARDT & ROTTERMANN,

Druggists and Apothecaries,

N. W. Cor. Third and St. Clair Sts.,

California Cough Balsam.
B. & R. Flavoring Extracts.
DAYTON, OHIO.

OSWALD CAMMANN,

General Insurance Agent.

Special attention given to placing fire insurance at the lowest possible rates in the best companies.

H. E. EMRICK,

HARDWARE

* * * * * * 15 South Main Street.

DUBOIS & SOWARD'S

City Music Store.

ESTABLISHED 1850.

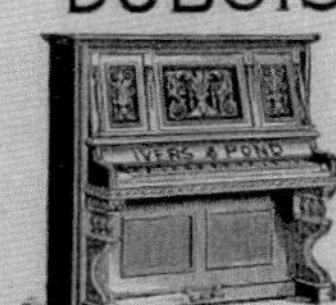

Pianos and all kinds of Musical Instruments, Strings, Sheet Music and Books.

21 South Main St. Opp. Market House.

J. SCHWAB & SON,

CIGARS,

7 South Main Street.

"A LEAF FROM AN OLD BOOK."

OUT of the past there comes to us a quaint little book, yellow with age, and of interest to us in our Centennial year. It is "The Harp of the West," a volume of poems by Joseph S. Welsh, Cincinnati, printed by Dawson and Fisher, 1839. The author does not "arrogate to himself the genius of Milton, of Homer, or of Pope." "His highest ambition is to plant in the bosoms of the rising generation the great, the good and ennobling principles of morality, virtue, and patriotism." The rising generation may thank Mr. Welsh for his thoughtful care, and for his giving to us in this far-away day a picture of our fair city in its earliest days.

One of the most interesting poems is "Recollections of Colonel Robert Patterson, Late of Dayton, Ohio." After giving many incidents in the life of Colonel Patterson, the poem closes with the following pen picture of early Dayton:

"Brave Patterson sought out a beauteous home;
And, lo! around, the wilderness did bloom
And blossom as the rose.
Near by him rose, from out the lonely waste,
A little village. I remember well
When heavy forests frowned along the streets
Of Dayton. And I 've often there beheld
The wild deer feeding 'neath the shady groves
Where now the buildings stand, and heard at night
The yell of the rapacious prowling wolf.
Of families some five or six dwelt round,
In little cabins; peace and friendship reigned
Uninterrupted 'mid the social group
Of active citizens. The blockhouse frowned
In murky grandeur o'er the river's brink
Just where the mouth of the main street doth meet
The water's edge. When night did shroud
This lonely hamlet, oft the dismal tale
Of savage cruelty would make the urchins crouch
To a close circle, round the blazing fire,
And while the blast moaned round the chimney-tops,
Think that they heard the foe advancing close
Upon their dwellings. Time can ne'er erase
Those first impressions and those early scenes
From off my memory—never can blot out
The traces of the friendship warm and sweet
That dwelt amid this little village band."

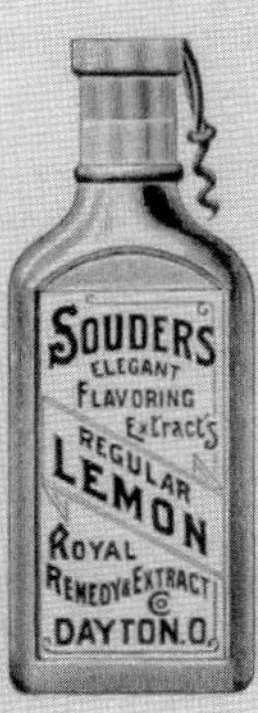

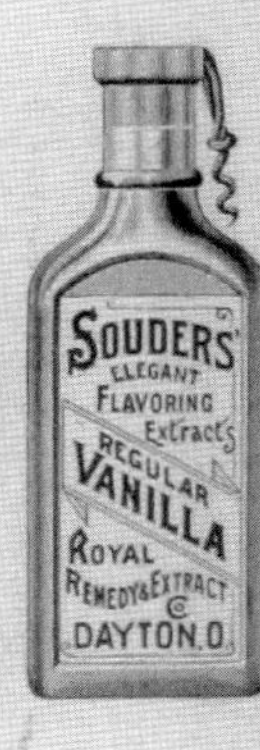

RIVERSIDE BREWERY.

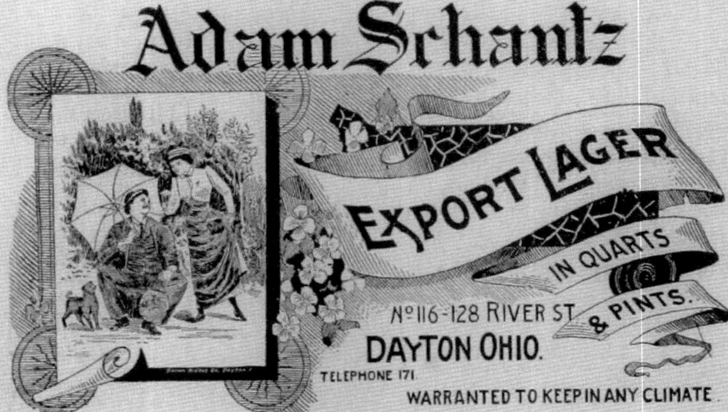

BREWER OF

Draught and Export Lager Beers,

UNEXCELLED AS A TONIC OR TABLE BEER.

25,203 Barrels of Beer sold during the year ending May 1, 1896, About 23,000 of which were sold in the city.

IN ORDER TO HAVE A GOOD, WHOLESOME BEER IT MUST HAVE AGE.

15,375 Barrels of Beer on hand May 1, 1896, more than any other two Brewers in the city.

* * * * * *

"SANDOW," THE STRONGEST MAN IN THE WORLD, on his recent visit to Dayton, drank Schantz's Beer and pronounced it the finest ever found in all his travels, covering almost the entire globe.

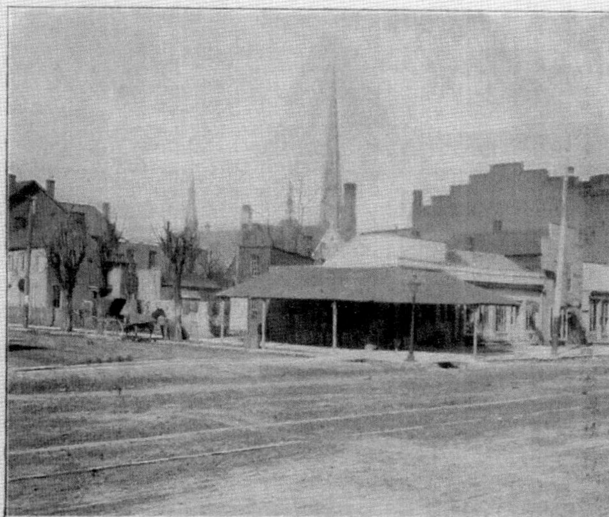

From "Early Dayton," by permission of the U. B. Publishing House.

NORTHWEST CORNER OF MAIN AND FOURTH STREETS IN 1882.

PRESENT SITE OF THE KUHNS BUILDING, THE CORNER BUILDING, ERECTED IN 1813, BEING THE OLDEST HOUSE SOUTH OF THIRD STREET.

"GENERAL HARRISON spent the 1st of September, 1812, in Dayton, and a salute of eighteen guns was fired in his honor. . . . The following appeal was sent to the ladies of Dayton from headquarters, St. Mary's, September 20, 1812: 'General Harrison presents his compliments to the ladies of Dayton and its vicinity, and solicits their assistance in making shirts for their brave defenders who compose his army.' . . . 'With a zeal and promptitude honorable to them and the State,' and, of course, without compensation, the ladies of Dayton immediately went to work, and by October 14 one thousand eight hundred shirts were ready to send to the army—a good deal of sewing to accomplish without the aid of a machine in less than four weeks by the women of a village of less than one hundred houses."

"On the 19th of May, 1813, the last number of the *Ohio Centinel* appeared, and for a year and five months no newspaper was published in Dayton. As a consequence, there is little material during this period for the history of the town."—*From "Early Dayton," published by the U. B. Publishing House.*

DAYTON OF THE PAST.

HARRIET M. KING.

IT is by contrast very often that we see the events of life in their most vivid light. It is the fashion now-adays to muse much over the forefathers who laid the foundation of our town, and we smile with quiet satisfaction as we fancy their grave eyes wandering over the modern city which we and time have evolved from their bit of a hamlet.

There is but little, after a hundred years, of material, tangible shape to show for those first, earliest days,—a log cabin by the riverside, a few old guns, pictures, bits of china, or furniture,—but the influence, the will, the character of the little group that slept under the trees here in the sweet spring weather a hundred years ago are closely woven into the Dayton of to-day.

It is pleasant to stop in our whirling life and recall their quiet, earnest personality, their independence and kindliness. What were their thoughts as they made paths through the woods, plowed their lands, built their simple homes, and laid out some of the streets on which we walk,—keeping always an eye open for redskins? Did they talk of the history which some of them had helped to make with the old gun in the corner, now loaded for wild beasts or treacherous Indians? What did they think of "The Terror" in France? What of Napoleon, who, while their pirogues were winding down the river, and their wagons pushing through the forests of Ohio, was leading his army into Italy, and so on towards the empire? Did their hearts burn over Poland's wrongs, so that they were more than half glad when a passing traveler brought word that great Catherine lay dead in Russia? Did they ever give the tribute of a homesick sigh to the comfort and security of the old English homes of their fathers? Men and women both had plenty of time to think, as they did their work in the quiet wilderness. Thoughts were turned over and over and well polished in those days. They were not a marketable commodity. There was no mania to rush them into print, or embalm them in ink.

A few adventurous spirits, accepting cheerfully and bravely for themselves the hard conditions of the life they had chosen, they built their brightest hopes upon the sons and daughters to whom they could leave the heritage of freedom in a pleasant land. And now they are sleeping — the "men whose lives glided on like rivers that water the woodlands, darkened by shadows of earth, but reflecting an image of heaven."

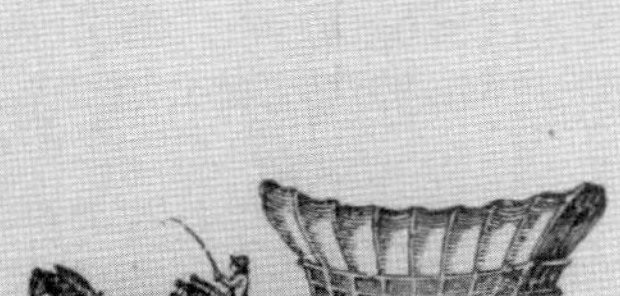

DAYTON WHEEL WORKS.

The Pinneo & Daniels Co.,

Manufacturers of

FINE

VEHICLE WHEELS,

DAYTON, OHIO.

GEORGE SCHANTZ, Pres.
LOUIS A. WEHNER, Sec'y.

The

Schantz & Schwind Brewing Co.,

Dayton, Ohio,

Brewers and Bottlers.

Telephone 176.

Foot of Perry Street.

N. Thomas,

HYDRAULIC BREWERY

AND

BOTTLING WORKS.

Cor. First and Beckel Sts. DAYTON, OHIO.

Established 1859.

R. P. BURKHARDT, PRES.
G. STOMPS, VICE-PRES. AND TREAS.
J. M. KRAMER, SEC'Y.
R. P. BURKHARDT, JR., SUP'T

THE STOMPS-BURKHARDT CO.,

Manufacturers of all Styles of

Chairs.

OFFICE AND FACTORY:
229 to 241 East First Street.

WAREROOMS:
126, 128, & 130 Canal Street.

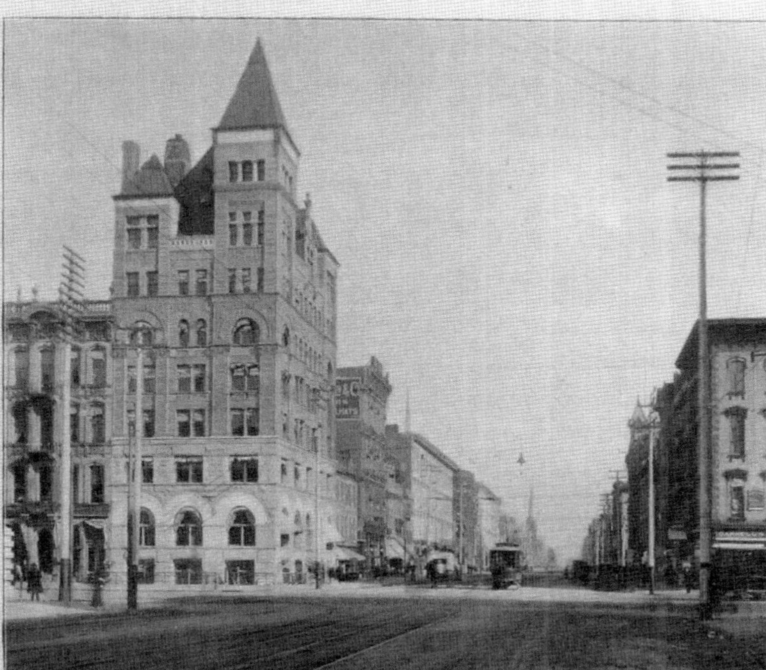

Callahan Bank Building.
From "Early Dayton," by permission of the U. B. Publishing House.

THIRD STREET, LOOKING EAST FROM MAIN.

"PERHAPS," in the language of Mary Davies Steele, "there is no impropriety in saying . . . of Dayton that no one living here who has undertaken literary, philanthropic, or other public work can help feeling that Dayton is a good place to live in, so ready is the response and generous the support and appreciation received. Thus, it seems to the student of our history, it has been from the beginning."

"WITHIN the last few years a complete sewer system has been projected and largely finished, and the principal streets of the city have been handsomely paved with asphalt, brick, sandstone, and granite; and many of the residence streets have been parked by narrowing the roadway and making lawns along the borders of the sidewalks. These improvements . . . make the streets very attractive."

BATES, ENGEL & COMPANY,

Ns. D. Bates. C. W. Engel.
Harry J. Rock. G. A. Heinz.

DRESS GOODS, SILKS, LADIES' AND MEN'S FURNISHERS,

"Largest Line of Popular-Price Dress Stuffs in this City."
Ladies' Ready Suits, Shirt Waists, and Dress Skirts on Third Floor.

106 E. Third and 10 & 12 S. Jefferson,
DAYTON, OHIO.

PHILIP J. ROTTERMAN,

Merchant Tailor,

No. 109 South Jefferson Street,
DAYTON, OHIO.

HELEN KEMPER & SISTER,

Dealers in

FANCY GOODS,

And all kinds of Working Materials, Laces, and Children's Caps.

113 North Main St., bet. First and Second Sts.

TURKISH and RUSSIAN

BATH HOUSE,

17 East Second Street,
Between Main and Second Streets.

Finest Equipped Bath House in the Western Country. Modern in Every Detail.

OPEN DAY AND NIGHT.

LADIES HOURS:
Mondays from 7 A.M. to 6 P.M.
Fridays from 7 A.M. to 1 P.M.

D. F. THOMPSON, Mgr.

Anderton & Eberhardt,

The "McCune" MEANS

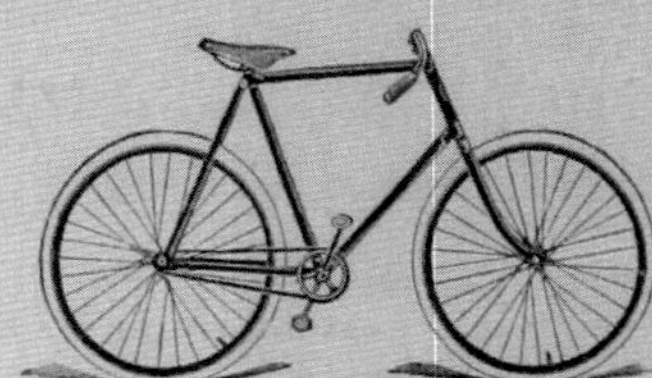

HIGH GRADE,
GRACEFUL FRAME,
GREATEST STRENGTH,
LIGHTEST FINISH,
LOWEST PRICE.

The Anderton & Eberhardt Co.,
General Agents,
18 NORTH MAIN STREET.

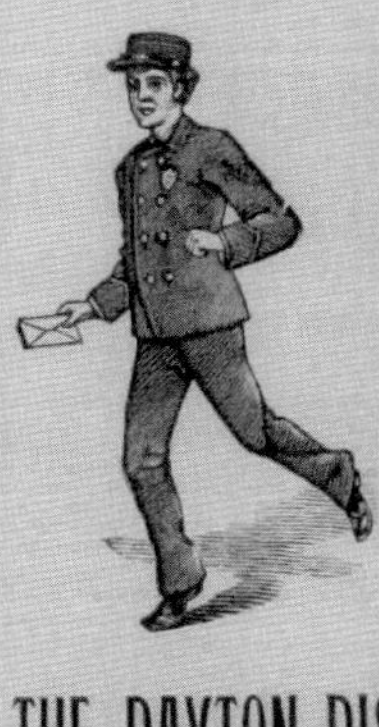

District Messenger Service.

Our messengers can be had at any hour, DAY or NIGHT, for all classes of errand duty.

THE DAYTON DISTRICT TELEGRAPH CO.,

18 S. JEFFERSON ST. PHONE 181.

THE SOUTHERN OHIO COAL CO.,

COAL AND COKE.

Telephone 378.

DAYTON OF THE PRESENT.

S. W. DAVIES.

DAYTON people have good cause to be proud of Dayton. The large outlay of the past few years has metamorphosed the city. We have broad, clean, well-lighted streets; excellent fire protection; abundance of the purest and coldest water; school buildings handsome in construction, admirably ventilated, heated, and lighted, with unused space for the coming scholars; a sewage system that has proved a success; more owners of homes than nine out of ten cities, and a steady-going, level-headed, progressive population. We have enough banking capital to help out our neighbors, and a large and growing building-association capital that has done more to build up the city with comfortable homes than any other factor.

In the gloom of the business depression we did not suffer above measure; we are not boomers and had built few air-castles. Solidity and steadiness are the characteristics of the leaders in manufacturing and merchandising. Primarily a manufacturing city, our name has gone out throughout the earth, and our products to the ends of the world.

We feed on the fat of the land. Fruits and vegetables, fresh from the adjacent country, fill our markets. You cannot buy better beef or mutton, pork or poultry, than are spread before the epicure triweekly.

Are you a reader? The riches of all ages are within the handsome library walls, free for the asking. Are you a social animal? Clubs, artistic, literary, religious, and non-religious, open wide their doors to men and women alike. Do you want to wear a uniform that would make a red Indian envious? Uniformed societies are endless.

The Dayton of to-day is beautiful, rich, powerful, and prosperous. We invite the stranger and sojourner to cast in his lot with us. We will help him if he is good, furnish a free bed in a splendid hospital if he is sick, put him in the new station-house if bad, and if he dies we will bury him in the most beautiful cemetery in the country. What reasonable man, alive or dead, could ask more?

TAKE A REST

IN OUR Solid Comfort Lawn Swing,

The most comfortable lounging place
for the hot days and nights.

RAKES, TEDDERS, LOADERS, MOWERS, CORN PLANTERS,
DISC HARROWS, GRAIN DRILLS, AND SEEDERS.

Every one the best of its class.
Our guaranty means something

Bicycles? Yes, for 1897.
Don't buy till you see ours.

STODDARD MFG. CO., DAYTON, OHIO.

THE COMPUTING SCALE CO.,

DAYTON, OHIO.

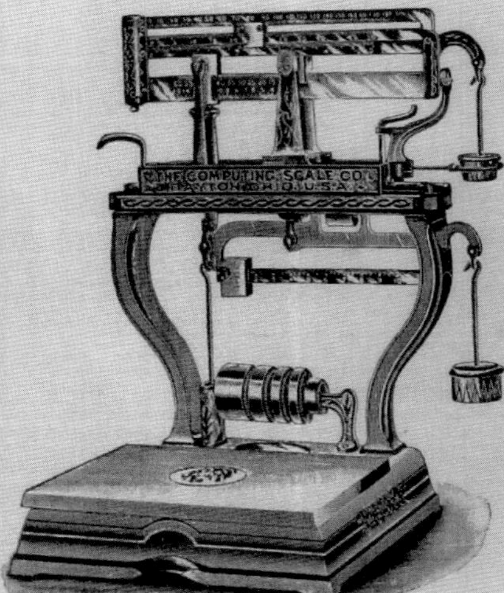

One of Dayton's Latest Enterprises.

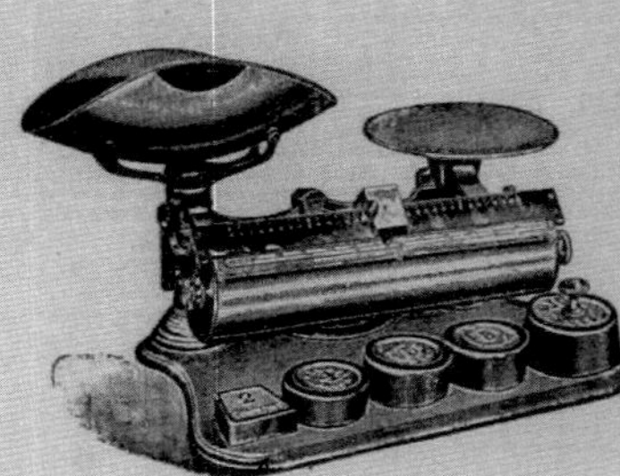

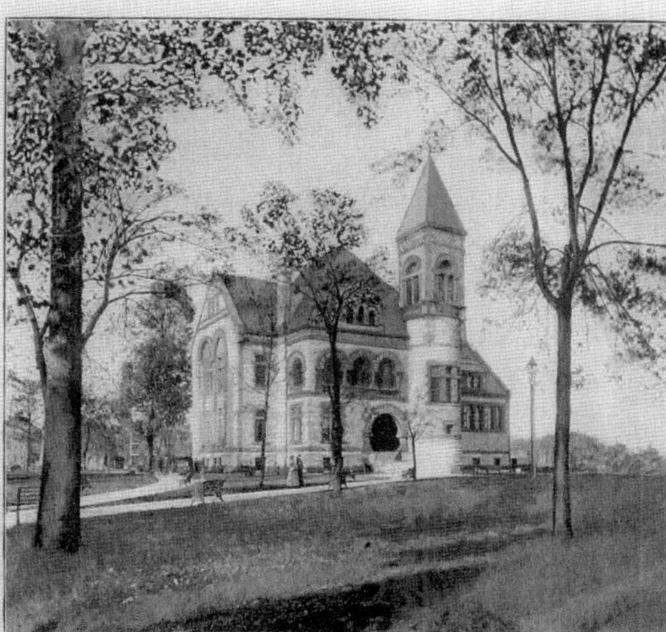

From "Early Dayton," by permission of the U. B. Publishing House.

PUBLIC LIBRARY AND MUSEUM, AND COOPER PARK.

ROBERT W. STEELE was one of the founders of the Dayton Library Association, and served for many years as director and president. After it was united with the Public Library in 1860, he was, excepting one or two years, till his death in 1891, a member of the Library Board. This Library united the strongest attachments of Mr. Steele—he loved his native town, and he loved his books. The Library contains 35,325 volumes and 1,292 pamphlets. Connected with the Library is a museum.

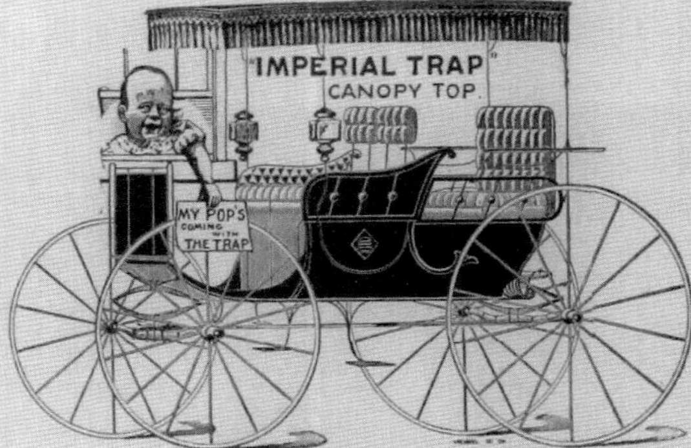

"A TRAP 'S THE THING!"

WE MAKE EIGHT VARIETIES OF

TRAPS,

BESIDES

SURREYS, PHAETONS, AND CABRIOLETS.

WE DO SELL AT RETAIL.

MORRIS WOODHULL,

FIFTH STREET, NEAR RIVER.

The Brownell & Co., Dayton, Ohio,

MANUFACTURERS OF

AUTOMATIC and THROTTLING ENGINES,

Saw Mills, Boilers of Every Description.

STAND PIPES, TANKS,

and General Sheet-Iron Work.

Send for Catalogue.

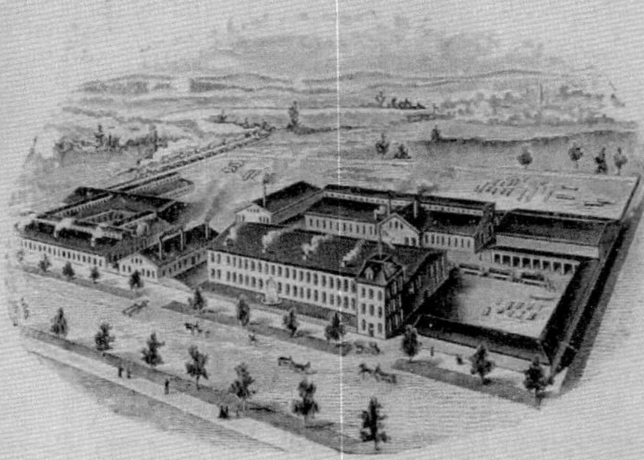

The Joyce-Cridland Co.,

Manufacturers of

Patent Lever, Compound-Lever, Screw, and

Hydraulic Jacks and Bench Vises.

Factory and Office, Cor. Wyandotte St. and R. R.

DAYTON OF THE FUTURE.

FRANK CONOVER.

WE have heard and read much in this Centennial year of the glories of Dayton's past; and we have congratulated our city and ourselves upon the greatness of her present. But of her future, who shall prophesy? It needs large faith and a facile pen to forecast the coming years.

The physical, material advancement of Dayton is very sure; her twenty years last past have not only been full of accomplishment, but have given a distinct impetus to our municipal growth which must be felt far into the future. Our industries will multiply; we will build great factories that shall dwarf those we think great to-day; our commercial relations with the outer world will expand, and our material wealth and prosperity will increase an hundred-fold. To the east, even to the hills, the valley will be filled with vast shops, employing capital and labor in harmonious coöperation, and their so-called conflict of to-day will have become ancient history. To the west, Dayton will crowd the gates of a great National Park, devoted only to the health and pleasure of the people, for wars will no longer furnish crippled veterans or soldiers' graves. From north to south this beautiful basin, the three-rivered valley, will scarce suffice to keep the Dayton of the future within her bounds.

This is not a foolish dream; it is but the faint shadowing of that which our children and their children will see.

But even better things than these shall be found in Dayton after a while.

A new sense of the high honor and grave responsibility of public service will prevail. The best citizens will give their best thought and labor to the public good. A rational, effective civil service system will govern Dayton, and honesty, integrity, capacity, not political creed, will test the right of every man to hold a place of public trust.

Great institutional churches will be a part of future Dayton's better life. These will be open every day, and they will educate the mind and strengthen the body, as well as minister to the spirit.

Every public school in Dayton will have its kindergarten, its natural history museum, its manual training department, its reference and circulating libraries.

If the Dayton of the future may not harbor a great university, she will at least have the benefits of university teaching brought to her doors, through the establishment, not of one Extension Center, but of twenty. The best in art, science, sociology, will be brought to her upon the tongues of the greatest thinkers and talkers of the world, for University Extension will become international, and Dayton will rank among the great centers of this magnificent plan for popular education.

These are but a meager hint of the things that shall be enjoyed in Dayton of the future.

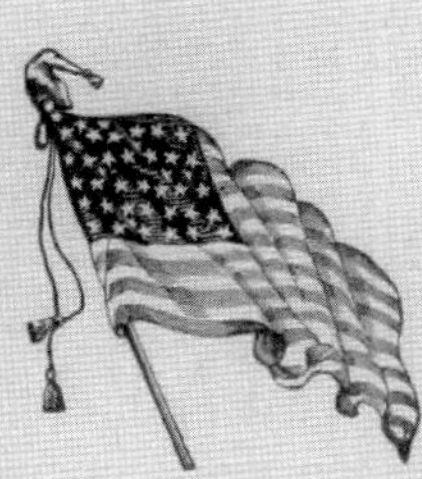

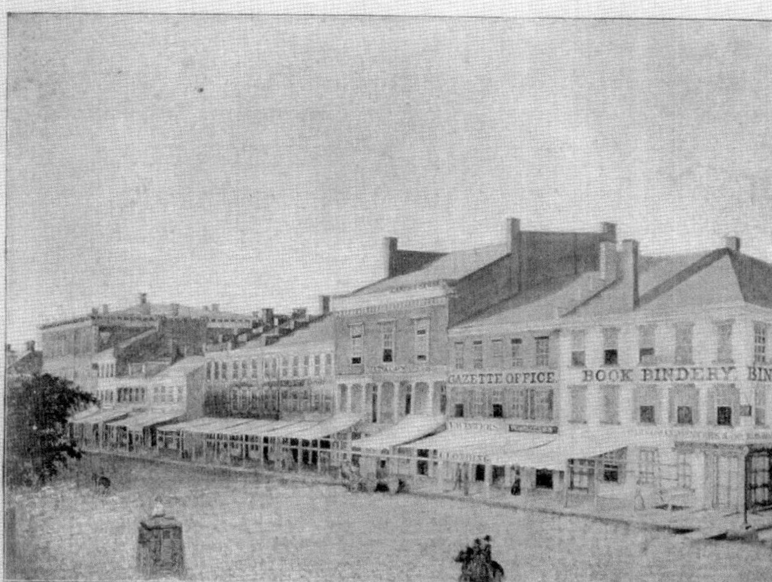

From a water-color painting by John W. Van Cleve, in possession of Miss Martha Holt.
From "Early Dayton," by permission of the U. B. Publishing House.

A VIEW OF THE EAST SIDE OF MAIN STREET, BETWEEN SECOND AND THIRD STREETS, IN 1855.

DAYTON owes much to the careful study and painstaking observation of Mr. John W. Van Cleve. This little picture brings before us the business of Dayton after it had come to a focus at the corner of Third and Main. These buildings contained the banks, newspaper, and stores. Dayton merchants kept genuine country stores, and sold a very miscellaneous variety of articles.

EARLY DAYTON

→

STEELE

Read the Special DAYTONIA Offer.

SPECIAL OFFER FOR DAYTONIA WEEK.

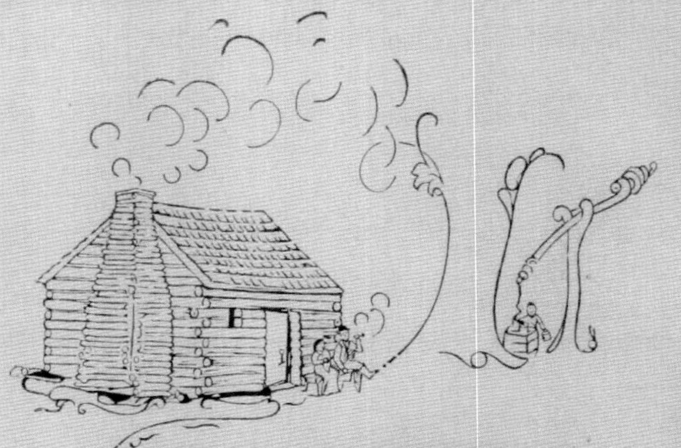

The Only History of Dayton from 1796 to 1896.
All Editions Completed.

EARLY DAYTON, a complete history of the first half-century, with important facts and incidents from the founding of the city of Dayton, Ohio, to the hundredth anniversary. 1796–1896. By Robert W. Steele and Mary Davies Steele. Illustrated. Acknowledged to be the best history of Dayton published—the *authoritative* history.

The best evidence of the excellence of this history is that since its publication in March it has been constantly quoted in public and private, and commended by every one who has had occasion to study the city's history. The orators and essayists at all the public occasions during the Centennial Celebration spoke of its importance and urged its use in every home in Dayton.

Used in planning DAYTONIA.

One of the best judges in the city says: "Miss Steele has narrated in a charming style the leading events in the history of Dayton. She has interwoven with her narrative biographical sketches of prominent participants in those events, thereby adding piquancy to the interest the subject would naturally excite in the minds of Daytonians. Every citizen should feel it to be not only a duty, but a pleasure, to become thoroughly acquainted with the facts set forth in 'Early Dayton.' The attractiveness of the volume is enhanced by admirable illustrations, faultless printing, excellent paper, and neat binding."

Three Editions are Issued:

CUT THIS OUT!

IT WILL BE GOOD FOR

10c. on the 60c. Edition,
20c. on the $1.25 Edition,
40c. on the $4.00 Edition,
of

EARLY DAYTON,

if presented at the

U. B. BOOK STORE,

Cor. Main and Fourth Sts.,

at any time between Monday, May 18, 1896, and Saturday Evening, May 23, 1896.

1.—Paper binding, thirty-eight illustrations, including scenes of early history, **$0.60.**

2.—Cloth binding, special design, with eighteen additional illustrations (a total of fifty-six), - - - - - - - - - - - - - - - **1.25.**

3.—Edition de Luxe, large paper, wide margins, gilt top, with nineteen special illustrations (a total of seventy-five), half leather binding, limited number, - - - - - - - - - - - - - - - - - **4.00.**

The last is the handsomest book of local history Dayton has had. It will prove valuable, as the number of copies is small and will not be increased.

The entire work is a home enterprise,—authorship, manufacture, sale, and all. It will remain the best monument in book form of Dayton's Centennial. Its publisher has desired to issue a book that could go into every home in the city. Hence the prices of the various editions are lower than for books of similar size and style.

If you cannot visit the Book Store and examine the books, a representative will call upon you.

United Brethren Publishing House,

Corner Main and Fourth Streets.

☞ **THE special offer named in the Coupon on this page will be good for the one week only. You want the book in your family. Buy it this week. It is a book to be kept and given to the children to be read as they grow older.**

"AUNTIE" BOYD.

ELIZA HOLT.

AMONG the names long associated with early Dayton, few are deserving of more kindly remembrance than that of Miss Maria Boyd, or "Auntie" Boyd, as she was sometimes familiarly called. The page assigned me is amply sufficient for any needed record of her life and character, much of which might be summed up in the single sentence, "She went about doing good." Her means, though limited, affording a competent support, she purchased a small home at the extreme end of First Street, where she resided till her death. Her family consisting only of a niece and a nephew, whom she had brought up from his infancy, enabled her to devote her time to the service which she loved. The almoner of others' bounty, as well as her own, she almost seemed to embody in her own person the associated charities of early Dayton. Long before those noble institutions, the St. Elizabeth and Deaconess Hospitals, were founded, the quaint little figure of Miss Boyd, peculiar in manner, dress, and appearance, might be daily seen, undeterred by winter's cold or summer's heat, carrying food to the hungry, clothing to the destitute, or comfort to the afflicted; or she might be met returning alone in the darkness of night from her errands of love and mercy. And not only could Miss Boyd encourage—she could reprove or rebuke when necessary.

A single incident may serve to show the secret of her happy life. On one occasion, calling at the house,—it must have been on some of her benevolent enterprises,—with a beaming face she exclaimed: "I was *so* happy for a few days, I was *so* happy. I did not know why I should feel so, but I thought it might be I was going to die." To die! think of it, any "who through fear of death" are "all their lifetime subject to bondage." For Miss Boyd to die was gain. Dying in 1879, for seventeen years Miss Boyd has been in the presence of the Master whom she served, and who, when on earth himself, said: "I was an hungered, and ye gave me meat: I was thirsty, and ye gave me drink: . . . . naked, and ye clothed me: I was sick, and ye visited me. . . . . Inasmuch as ye have done it unto one of the least of these my brethren, ye have done it unto me."

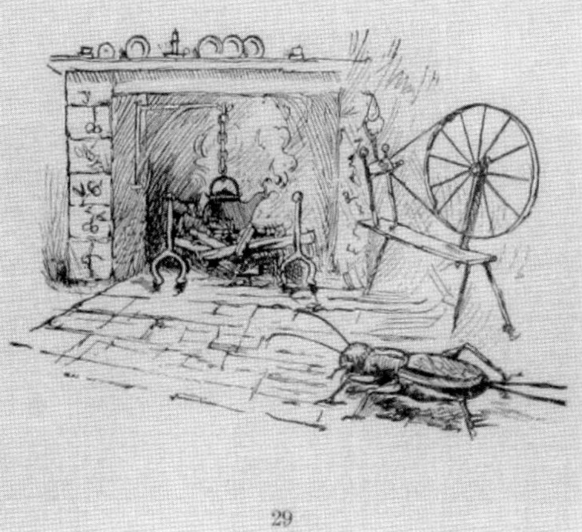

Try Our

NEW DRIFTED SNOW FLOUR.

JOSEPH R. GEBHART & SON.

McKEMY & NUTT,

ATTORNEYS AT LAW.

ROOMS 9, 10, and 11, KUHNS BLDG.,

Corner Main and Fourth Streets.

Telephone No. 690.

JOHN HANITCH,

ATTORNEY AT LAW,
NOTARY PUBLIC.

18 E. Third St., - DAYTON, O.

THIRD NATIONAL BANK,

DAYTON, OHIO.

UNITED STATES DEPOSITORY.

Capital, - - - - - $400,000.00
Surplus and Net Profits, - 140,911.66

JOHN K. McINTIRE, Pres. CHAS. RENCH, Cash.
RUFUS J. KING, V.-Pres. CHAS. J. MOORE, Asst. Cash.

A General Banking Business Transacted.

FOR GOOD CLOTHING AT LOWEST PRICES

GO TO

SOL STRAUSS,

THE LEADING

CLOTHIER, HATTER, AND FURNISHER,

28 and 30 E. Third St.,
23 and 25 N. Market St., DAYTON, OHIO.

THE DAYTON PAPER NOVELTY CO.,

INCORPORATED.

MANUFACTURERS OF **PATENT PAPER PACKAGES.**

232 to 256 E. First Street,
125 to 141 N. Mill Street, DAYTON, OHIO, U. S. A.

BENJ. F. McCANN,

ATTORNEY AT LAW.

24 North Main Street, - DAYTON, OHIO.

Telephone 958.

RIKE'S.

Identified for nearly half a century with Dayton's every advancement and reform.

THE RIKE DRY GOODS CO.,

MAIN AND FOURTH STREETS.

We solicit a continuance of your favors.

A. GEBHART, President. E. A. DANIELS, Vice-President. A. S. ESTABROOK, Cashier. THOS. GABLE, Assistant Cashier.

The Merchants National Bank, ODD FELLOWS TEMPLE.

Receives Deposits. Discounts Acceptable Paper. Issues Their Own Drafts on Foreign Places. Capital, $300,000. Surplus, $60,000.

DIRECTORS: A. GEBHART, J. H. VAILE, J. LINXWEILER, JR., J. C. PEIRCE, A. J. CONOVER, A. GERLAUGH, E. A. DANIELS, G. C. KENNEDY, SOL. RAUH.

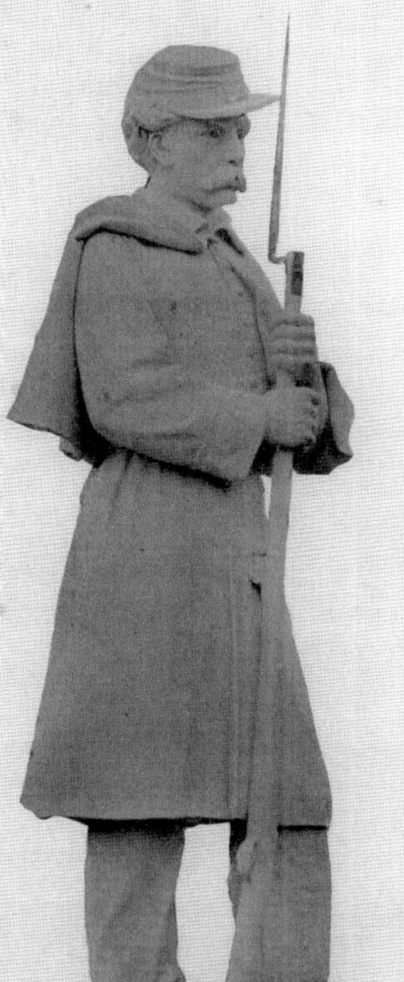

STATUE SURMOUNTING THE SOLDIERS' MONUMENT.

"The memorial of Montgomery County to her soldiers" was dedicated July 31, 1884. Total height of the monument is 85 feet. The model for the statue, which is 11 feet 6 inches in height, was George Fair of the regular army.

The Wheel in 1796.

She sat beside her spinning-wheel
  Demure and sweet and wise,
The golden sunshine on her hair,
  Love's language in her eyes.
Young Robert paused to note her skill—
  The capture was complete,
For she who turns the spinning-wheel
  Brings lovers to her feet.

The Wheel in 1896.

She sits upon her STEARNS wheel,
  Coquettish, witty, fair;
The bloom of health is on her cheek,
  The sunlight on her hair.
Young Edward's wheel keeps pace with hers
  Past field and forest wide,
For she who rides a STEARNS wheel
  Brings lovers to her side.

WE SELL THEM.

The Dayton Cycle Co.,

20 WEST SECOND STREET.

☞ *Exclusive Agency.*

Troy Laundry

405, 407, 409
East Third Street.

Our work
is simply
out of sight.

Call us up by Telephone
587 and 160.

Reed, Kelly & Co.

The Pearl Laundry Co.,

THOS. A. SELZ, Manager.

106, 108, 110 East Second Street.

· Telephone 581.

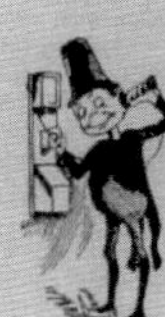

BEST WORK IN THE CITY.

Full line of Sundries.
First-class Repairing.
Telephone 815.

Gem City Cycle Co.

CLIFFORD R. BOUCK, Mgr.

No. 5 East Second Street.

THISTLE, WARWICK,
VANGUARD, ALLEN,
GEM SPECIAL,
  And a full line of
  medium grade wheels.

The ELYRIA JUVENILE,
  strongest, easiest running,
  and handsomest child's
  wheel made.

DAYTON IN THE WAR.

GENERAL SAMUEL BACON SMITH.

WHEN the proclamation of the President calling for the immediate enlistment of seventy-five thousand soldiers for a service of three months was received, Dayton responded with cheerfulness and alacrity, and within a very few days five companies of infantry were sworn into the service of the United States, and at least that many more were refused. These companies were attached to the First and Eleventh regiments. The First Regiment was mustered in at Lancaster, Pennsylvania, April 29, 1861, with Dayton men as officers, as follows: Lieutenant-Colonel Edwin A. Parrott, Major John G. Hughes, Adjutant Joseph S. Parrott, Regimental Quartermaster James Steele, and Captains Peter Dister, Louis Kuhlman, Walter B. Pease, and John Crowe. The Eleventh Regiment was mustered in at Columbus, Ohio, April 26, 1861, the Dayton officers being Colonel J. Findlay Harrison and Captains Calvin J. Childs and Michael P. Nolan.

At the end of its term the First Ohio was returned to Dayton to be recruited for a term of three years. The organization was completed, and it went to the field in the fall of 1861 with the following Dayton men as officers: Lieutenant-Colonel Edwin A. Parrott, Adjutant John Parrott, Captains Louis Kuhlman, Gates P. Thruston, and Patrick O'Connell.

Dayton claimed proprietorship in three infantry regiments, namely, the First, Eleventh, and Ninety-third. The Eleventh was recruited for three years at Camp Dennison and sent to West Virginia. It was, however, afterwards a part of the Army of the Cumberland and participated in some of its important battles, including Chickamauga.

The Ninety-third Regiment was organized at Dayton in the summer of 1862, its Dayton officers being as follows: Colonel Charles Anderson, Lieutenant-Colonel Hiram Strong, Assistant-Surgeon J. M. Weaver, Adjutant Dickenson P. Thruston, and Chaplain Osman A. Lyman, with Captains W. H. Martin, William Birch, Thomas C. Mitchell, and Samuel B. Smith.

Besides the organizations above mentioned Dayton was represented in numerous regiments of infantry, artillery, cavalry, heavy artillery, sharpshooters, etc., by companies, squads, and recruits, some of her citizens participating in nearly every battle of the War. From the 1st of September, 1862, until September 24, 1864, when the term of the First Regiment expired, the First and Ninety-third regiments were attached to the same brigade and side by side confronted the enemy at Stone River, Chickamauga, Chattanooga, Mission Ridge, Buzzard's Roost, Resaca, Kenesaw Mountain, and Atlanta.

In the suppression of the great Rebellion it is sufficient to say that the city of Dayton was in no way behind her sister cities in this and other Northern States in her manifestations of patriotism and that she freely and cheerfully contributed her sons to the army, her daughters to the care of the wounded and suffering, and her means, in generous quantity, to the support of the Government.

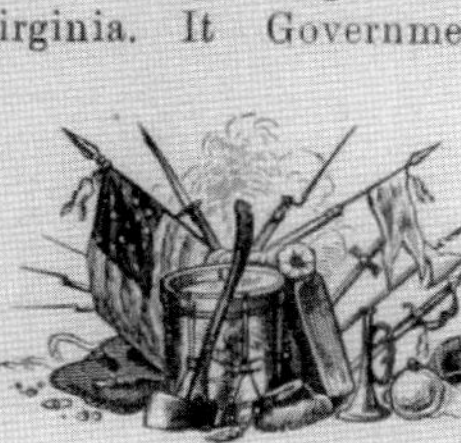

Best Clothes *and* **Hats.**

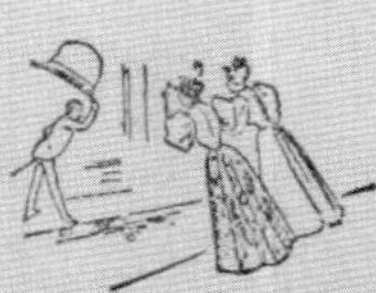

Best Fixings, *all* **Kinds.**

MOSE COHEN & CO., THIRD STREET.

ESTABLISHED 1861. LEE R. HOOPER, PRES.

DAYTON AWNING AND TENT CO

33 NORTH JEFFERSON ST.

MANUFACTURERS OF

Awnings, Tents, Paulins, and All Kinds of Canvas Work. Sidewalk Canopies, Floor Covers, and Tents Rented.

D. G. PORTER,

∴ DENTIST, ∴

26 North Jefferson Street, - DAYTON, OHIO.

Simms Building, Opposite Beckel House.

HARRY H. PRUGH,

Attorney and Counselor at Law.

Rooms 12 and 13 Kuhns Building, Fourth and Main Streets, DAYTON, O.

H. L. HUBER. W. D. HUBER.

HUBER BROTHERS,

AUCTIONEERS AND STORAGE WAREHOUSEMEN,

14, 16, and 18 S. Jeff. St., Telephone 786. DAYTON, OHIO.

FRED. REIBOLD, President. EDW. PAPE, SR., Vice-President. JOS. SCHUMACHER, Cashier.

THE TEUTONIA NATIONAL BANK,

DAYTON, OHIO.

Capital, $200,000. Surplus, $26,000.

W. W. FERGUSON. J. A. PRITZ. F. B. ROOP.

THE ACME STAR STEAM LAUNDRY.

WORKS AND MAIN OFFICE, 38 South St. Clair Street

Telephone 1129.

CRESCENT BICYCLES!

SKY HIGH.

PRICES: $40, $50, and $75.

W. E. HAAS & CO., 20 WEST FIFTH STREET.

THE EQUITABLE LOAN AND SAVINGS ASSOCIATION,

No. 8 NORTH JEFFERSON STREET.

DIRECTORS :

L. C. EVANS, M. COSTELLO, N. THOMAS, S. E. KUMLER, W. H. HOFFMAN, C. E. SPINDLER, THOS. De ARMON.

Dyeing and Cleaning.

Ladies' Dresses, Men's Clothing, Silks, Satins, Plushes, Portieres, Gloves, Parasols, Etc.

DAYTON CLEANING AND REPAIR CO., E. R. Lines, Mgr.

Phone 1070. *37 WEST FOURTH STREET.*

G. W. SHROYER & CO.

HAVE

GOOD BICYCLES.

23 W. FIFTH STREET.

DRINK O-R COFFEE!

Roasted by an Improved Process.

A Special Blend of High Grade Coffees. Packed in One Pound Cartons Only. Sold by All Grocers at **30 Cents Per Pound.**

DAYTON SPICE MILLS CO., ROASTERS.

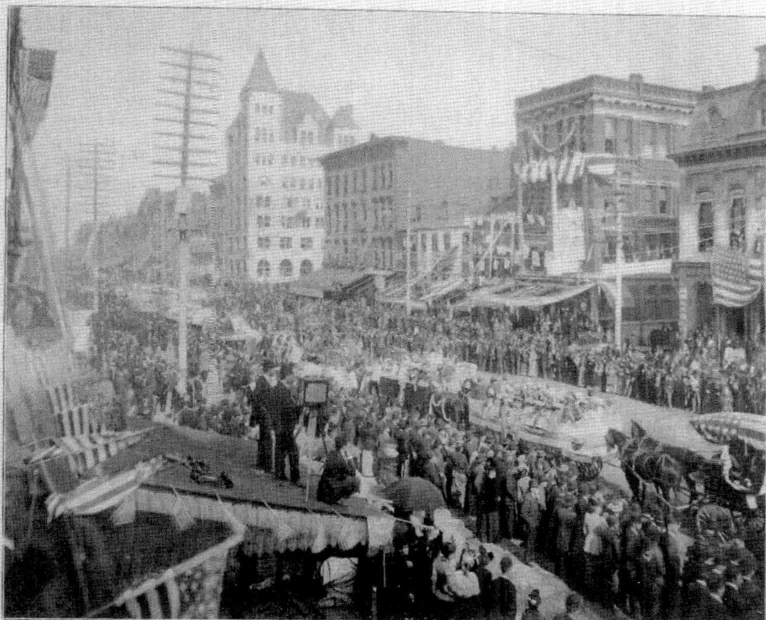

From "Early Dayton," by permission of the U. B. Publishing House.

COLUMBIAN CENTENNIAL, OCTOBER 22, 1892—A VIEW OF THE PROCESSION ON MAIN STREET.

On the 22d of October, 1892, the Columbian Centennial was fittingly celebrated in Dayton by an immense procession of military and civic societies, school-children, and industrial exhibits, followed by appropriate addresses and music in Cooper Park.

No language can describe the mammoth parade, which contained within itself the best evidence, not only of the wonderful progress of the hundred years preceding, but also of the magnificent manufactories and business enterprises of our city.

The addresses were worthy of the occasion, and the singing of "My country, 't is of thee," by the school-children was most inspiring, and wrought up the immense multitude to a high pitch of enthusiasm.

"The voice of gratitude and praise for all the blessings which have been showered upon mankind by Columbus's adventure is limited to no language, but is uttered in every tongue. Neither marble nor brass can fitly form his statue. Continents are his monument, and unnumbered millions, present and to come, will preserve his name and fame."

The M. Ohmer's Sons Co.

WE ARE now ready to see you at our New Store, Corner Main and Fifth Streets.

THE FINEST SALESROOMS,

THE FINEST STOCK OF FURNITURE IN THE STATE.

Our Upholstering and Repairing Departments are on the sixth floor and we are prepared to do over your old furniture on short notice.

Prices Remain the Lowest.

The M. OHMER'S SONS CO.,
Corner Main and Fifth Streets.

THE "INSURANCE" GASOLINE STOVE.

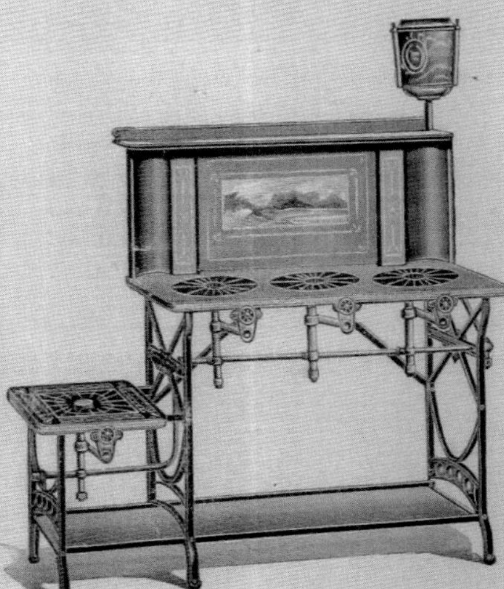

SIMPLEST!
SAFEST!
BEST!

YOU CANNOT

EXPLODE IT!

No Treacherous Drip Cups.
Lights with a Torch
Automatic Cut-Off Burner.

SEE IT BEFORE PURCHASING!

MADE BY THE DAYTON MANUFACTURING CO.

THE INDUSTRIES OF DAYTON.

E. M. THRESHER.

IN the industries of a city we find the sum of its enterprise, intelligence, and thrift added to the opportunities of its environment. The same natural causes which made the beautiful Miami Valley accessible to its first settlers gave them also ready means of communication with other markets, where the surplus products of their labor and skill might be exchanged for the comforts and luxuries there obtainable.

When our pioneers landed their pirogue at the mouth of Mad River they found here a healthful and beautiful location, a productive soil, an available supply of power to turn the wheels of their manufactories, and ready means of communication with outside markets. The same natural causes which led them to this favored spot also brought to their doors the canal and railroad when the time came that the packet must supplant the flat-boat and the pirogue, itself in turn to be replaced by the lightning express. From the time that the completion of the Miami and Erie canal gave to Dayton its splendid water-power there has been a steady growth of its industries, until we see to-day the prosperous Gem City, with its 80,000 inhabitants, and its productions known in all the States and in other continents.

Besides the usual jobbing trades and local industries of a thriving city, Dayton possesses large wholesale establishments in the lines of groceries, dry goods, spices, confections, millinery, books, stationery, and other commodities. It has for years been favorably and widely known for its manufacture of railroad cars, agricultural implements, wood, iron, cotton, clay-working and paper-making machinery, linseed oil, paints, varnishes, oil presses, water-wheels, pumps, gas and steam engines, boilers, iron and brass castings, electrical machinery, cash registers, computing scales, carriages, flour, paper and cardboard, ale and beer, lasts and pegs, boots and shoes, wood and paper boxes, bookbinders' machinery, wheels, hubs and spokes, sewing-machines, bicycles, stoves and castings, builders' supplies, furniture, lard oil, candles and soap, flavoring extracts, tobacco, toilet articles, business stationery, newspapers, books and periodicals, and many other young and growing industries. Its biscuits and crackers are famous, as are its pills and tonics, and it furnishes in many kinds remedies for all ills that man is heir to.

In the wide diversity of its manufactures lies one of the chief sources of our city's present strength and future promise. It is generally conceded that the proposed Centennial Exhibit of the manufactures of Dayton will be a revelation to the public, who have little idea of the extent, perfection, and variety of its products.

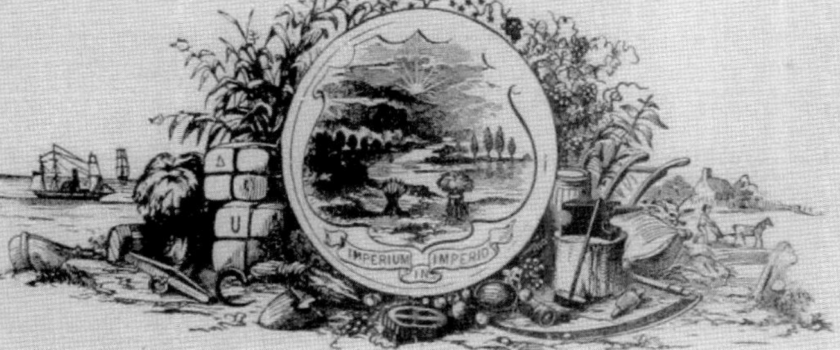

DAYTON—THE CITY OF CHURCHES.

H. F. COLBY, D.D.

THE count made on April 1, in this Centennial year, shows that Dayton has 81 churches, or public places of worship. Of these 71 are Protestant, 7 Catholic, and 3 Jewish. The whole population of Dayton is about 80,000. Now, if we bear in mind that infants, the sick and infirm, those temporarily absent, and those engaged in more or less necessary Sunday labor must be deducted from the number of church attendants; if we add to the places of worship reported the services held at the Young Men's Christian Association, the Woman's Christian Association, the Widows' Home, the Asylum for the Insane, the Catholic and Protestant hospitals, and other places; especially, if we remember that each of the churches holds several services on Sunday and during the week, it is evident that the proportion of public religious privileges to the population is very large, and that no one in the city need go far to find a place of worship congenial to his convictions and tastes.

Many of the churches are commodious and elegant structures, ornaments to our city, as well as constant invitations to higher things. Among the congregations referred to are 12 Methodist, 11 Baptist, 11 United Brethren, 9 Presbyterian, 7 Lutheran, 6 Reformed, 3 Episcopal, and 12 other denominations of one or two congregations each. In matters of common Christian interest all these have for a long time worked together with the greatest harmony and good feeling. Indeed, while every thoughtful Christian must have his own denominational preferences, our community has been singularly free from those jealousies and antagonisms which develop sectarian bitterness.

Of our 80,000 people, 30,604 are reported as belonging to some religious organization. On the morning of Easter Sunday the congregations aggregated 26,392, besides many children in the Sunday schools who did not attend the other services. In the Sunday schools there were 14,459. The various church property is valued at $1,858,315. The amount raised for church expenses in 1895 was $182,409, and the amount given by the churches to benevolence and charity was $107,538. Aside from the bearing of these things upon spiritual consolations and the hopes of the future, who can estimate their influence upon the morality, integrity, and mutual confidence of our citizens? Such a city of churches can be "no mean city," if those churches are faithful to their work.

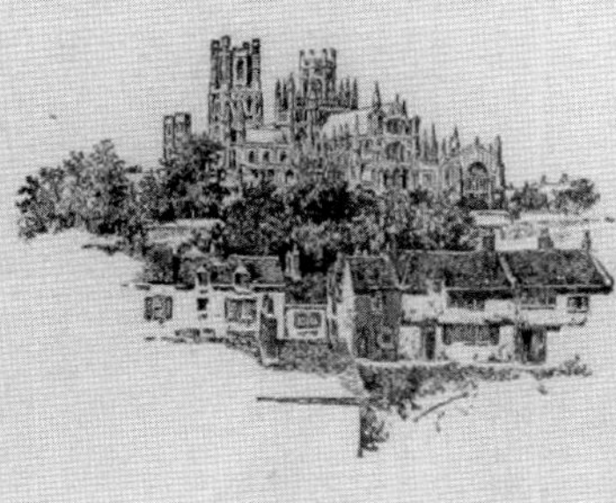

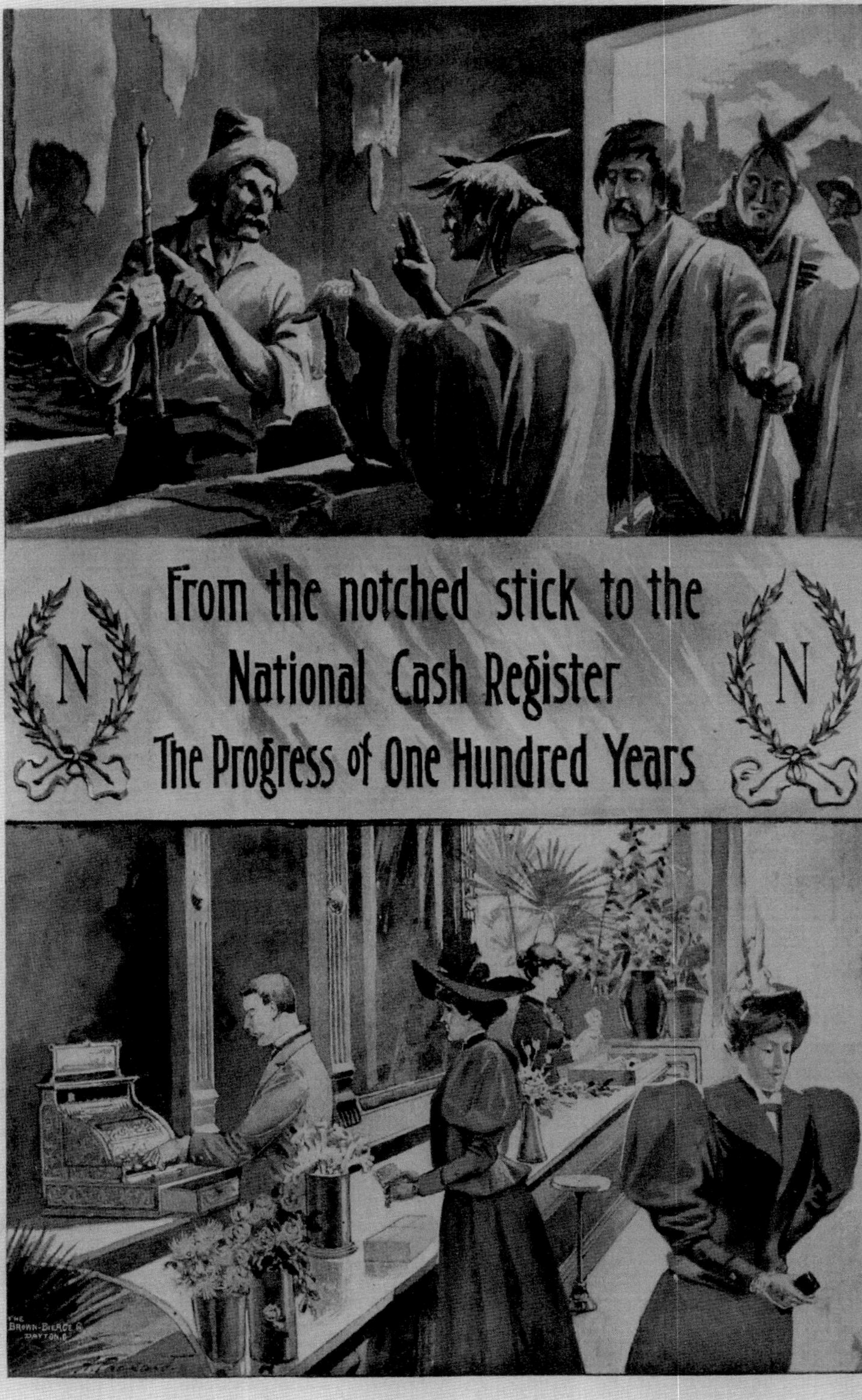
From the notched stick to the
National Cash Register
The Progress of One Hundred Years
N
N

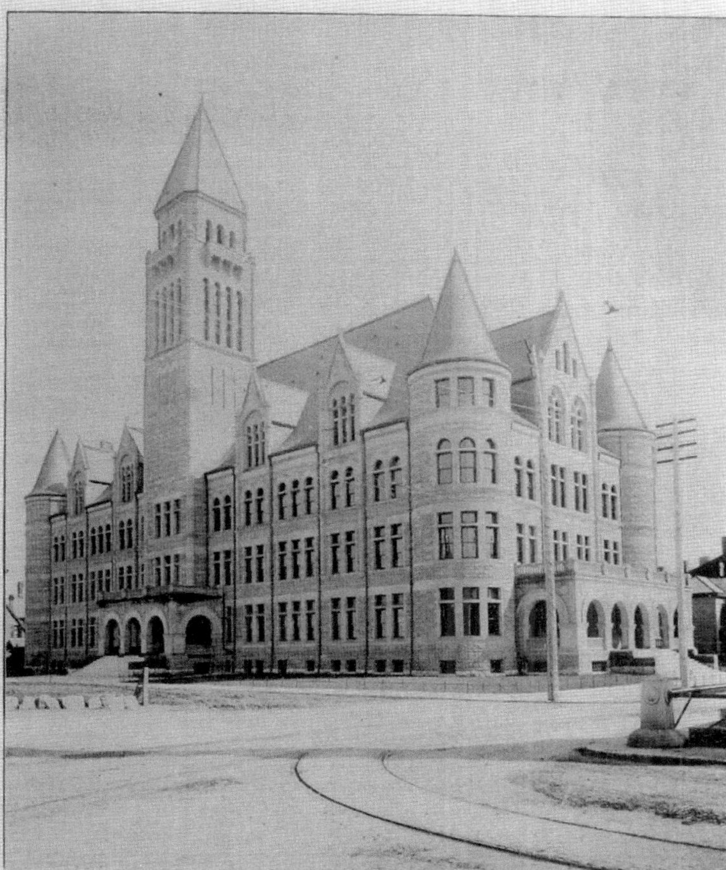

STEELE HIGH SCHOOL.

"In the spring of 1850, the Central High School of Dayton was opened. In the fall it was located in the old academy building, where it remained until 1857, when a new building was put up for it on the same ground—on the southwest corner of Fourth and Wilkinson streets. . . . Since then the roll of teachers and pupils has lengthened, and the curriculum broadened, but the same spirit of zeal, energy, and enthusiasm rules in the new High School building, occupied since 1892, and named in honor of one of the best friends of the schools—Robert W. Steele."—*From "Early Dayton."*

SEIDL & MERKLE,

Dealers in BOOTS, SHOES, and RUBBERS.

25 East Third Street.

Sign of the Wire Boot.

D. LEONHARD & SON,

Dayton's
Oldest and Best SADDLERY HOUSE.

You are all invited to call on them.

25 South Main Street. DAYTON, OHIO.

BOSLER'S BAKERY,

40 SOUTH MAIN STREET.

J. T. DRYDEN,

STAPLE AND FANCY GROCER.

Main and Second.

Telephone 521.

OWENS & HIXSON

MAKE SHIRTS
THAT FIT.

C. L. G. BREENE,

MERCHANT
TAILOR.

7 North Jefferson St. DAYTON, O.

S. B. WILLIAMS,

The Leading HATTER and FURRIER.

Telephone 495.

10 North Main Street.

H. N. WILES & CO.,

20 East Third St.,

DRY GOODS, WRAPS, ETC.

PRUDEN'S FAIR,

HOUSE FURNISHING GOODS, BABY CARRIAGES, AND REFRIGERATORS.

Novelties for Presents.

4 & 6 East Fifth Street. Pruden's Building.

You can get anything you may need to furnish your home at

BYRNE & PALMER'S,

111 East Third Street.

Cash or Credit.

CARNELL'S,

S. E. Corner Third and Main Streets.
An Up-to-Date
DRUG STORE.

CENTRAL WINE DEPOT.

WILLIAM SANDER,

Foreign and Domestic Wines and Liquors

Telephone 585.
Corner Third and St. Clair Streets.

CROSLEY & ADAMSON,

WHOLESALE GROCERS,

117 East Third Street, Dayton, Ohio.

Huffman Block.

JOS. FERNEDING & CO.,

Dealers in FINE BOOTS and SHOES.

34 East Third Street,
DAYTON, OHIO.

THE PUBLIC SCHOOLS OF DAYTON.

E. L. SHUEY.

IN this Centennial year there are about 11,000 children and youth in the public schools of Dayton. Of this number nineteen-twentieths will receive all their education in these schools. The very small proportion remaining will have more or less of the training of the college or technical school. Not one thousand of the eleven thousand are in the High School. About ninety-eight hundred are under fifteen years of age. For the instruction of these youth the city employs a superintendent, twenty-six high-school, four special, and nearly three hundred district-school teachers.

These facts only serve to emphasize the importance of a well-rounded course of study, broadly planned and carefully extended, in order that there may be the widest possible training for the great majority whose education is to be so limited, as well as the greatest encouragement and most thorough instruction for those who are to have the more advanced opportunities of the High School. That instruction only will be adequate which best fits the child for his environment and gives to him the incentive for the most complete development of himself. That this can no longer be limited to the "three R's" is fully demonstrated, and the question ought to be more fully appreciated by parents and instructors alike.

In nothing is the contrast of the hundred years more striking than in the requirements of education. Where success in almost any calling was assured to him who with the most elementary education united good judgment, now even the least calling requires a good knowledge of many subjects, and the higher positions in mechanic and mercantile pursuits alike demand training of head and hand.

Above all this, there must be in all schools that instruction in the history and genius of our country and its government, that sense of honor and responsibility for its control, that love of home and its duties, which will make the boys and girls of to-day a strong generation, truth-loving, independent in thought, and always loyal to home and country. Only as these elements are firmly fixed in the youth, do the schools of Dayton fulfill the proper demands of its citizens.

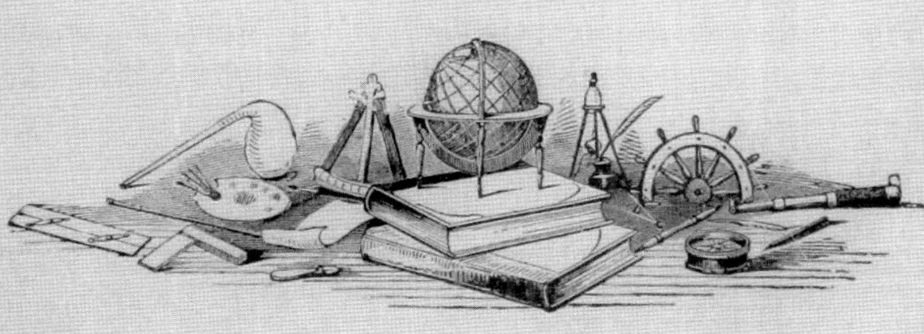

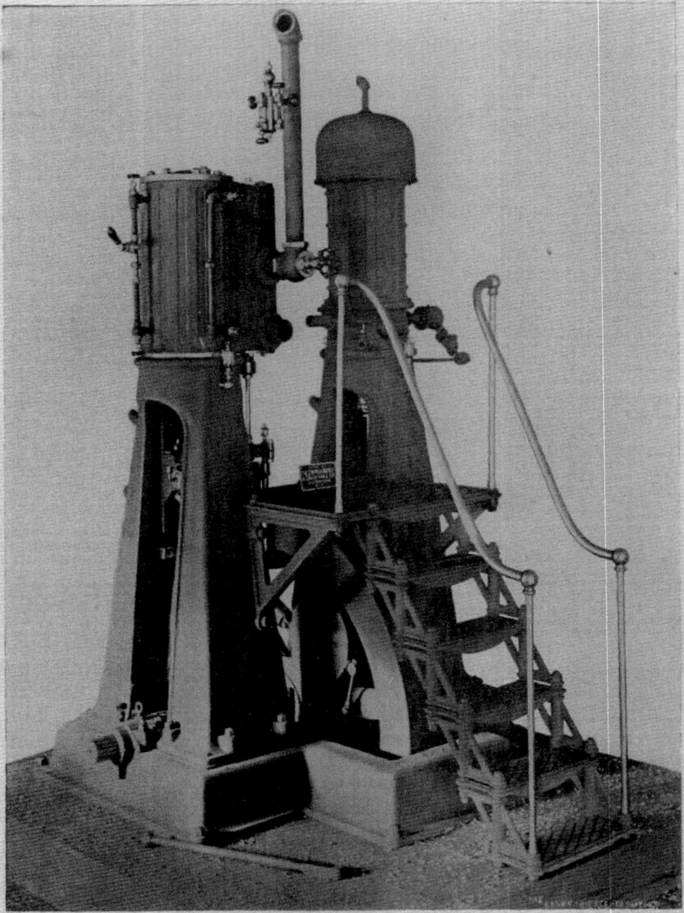

The "VICTOR" Ice and Refrigerating Machine.

A THOROUGHLY first-class machine of small to medium capacity, at moderate cost, especially adapted for Hotels, Hospitals, Butchers, Dealers in Fruits, Vegetables, Fish, Etc.

WE also manufacture on a large scale Turbines, Steam Pumps, Oil-Mill Machinery, Feed-Water Heaters, Filter Presses, Power-Transmitting Machinery, Etc.

ILLUSTRATED CATALOGUE ON APPLICATION.

The Stilwell-Bierce & Smith-Vaile Co.,

DAYTON, OHIO.

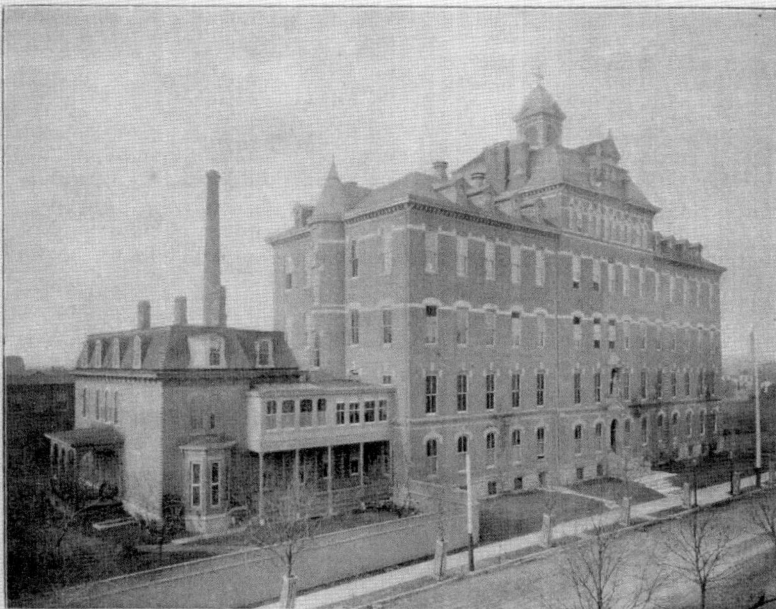

From "Early Dayton," by permission of the U. B. Publishing House.

ST. ELIZABETH HOSPITAL.

"THE St. Elizabeth Hospital is a Roman Catholic institution, which was started on Franklin Street, in 1878, in a very modest way by two Sisters of the Poor of St. Francis. They soon found that there was a broad field for their work. More room was needed. Six acres of land in Browntown were purchased, and the corner-stone laid in 1881 for a large building. There, supported by voluntary contributions, they are doing a noble work. Capacity, 242 patients."

ST. ELIZABETH HOSPITAL.

FATHER CHARLES A. KEMPER.

ST. ELIZABETH HOSPITAL, which now forms an imposing aggregation of buildings on the western bank of the Miami, in Browntown, had its very humble beginning in a two-story brick house on Franklin Street, near Ludlow. Next to God, its founding is chiefly due to the zeal, wisdom, and personal sacrifices of the late Rev. J. F. Hahne. As pastor of Emanuel's congregation, this saintly man clearly recognized the crying need of a hospital in our large city, and repeatedly made futile efforts to realize his hopes and prayers for its establishment. When at last, on July 2, 1878, two Franciscan sisters arrived from Cincinnati to undertake the work, they came at his solicitation, and assumed full control of the unpretentious yet neat house he had leased and prepared for their occupancy.

The first patient received in the original St. Elizabeth Hospital was an accident case—a poor brakeman, whose arm had been frightfully crushed in the yards about the depot. The work once begun, the number of applications for admission increased so rapidly that it soon became painfully evident how utterly inadequate to the demands made upon it were the accommodations of the Franklin Street house. Accordingly, after much prayer and consultation, and with scarce any funds save an unlimited fund of trust in the Father of the poor and in the generosity of the people of Dayton, the sisters purchased the site whereon was built the present roomy and splendidly equipped edifice, which was formally dedicated on Nov. 19, 1882. To the main structure other smaller buildings were in time added, either by purchase or erection, specially noticeable among the latter kind being what is called "St. Ann's House," whose purpose it is to receive, whenever necessary, such cases as require isolation or special treatment.

St. Elizabeth Hospital has already had an existence of nearly eighteen years. During that period fully fifteen thousand patients, afflicted with almost every form of suffering to which the human family is liable, have been nursed within its walls, no question as to creed, color, nationality, or pay being ever asked to determine the admission.

God alone can estimate what a record of unselfish devotion on the one hand, and of alleviated suffering on the other, is contained in these cold figures of its age and beneficiaries; and from him, surely, came the inspiration that moved the projectors of DAYTONIA to resolve that the proceeds of this part of Dayton's Centennial celebration should be equally divided between two institutions which, for their structural excellences, their monumental testimony to the generosity of our citizens, and their silent but eloquent evidence of Christ-like service done by sisters and unsalaried medical staff, are not the least of many reasons why Dayton proudly celebrates her first centenary.

PROGRAM.

SCENE I, 1796.

Our Grandmother in Newcom's Log Cabin Laboriously Making One Shirt in One Day.

SCENE II, 1886 TO 1896.

Ten Years of the Century Just Closing Devoted to the Developing and Perfecting of

GARMENT MANUFACTURE

IN THE GEM CITY

Under Our Namesake's Trade Mark

The Gem

TRADE MARK

SCENE III, MAY, 1896.

DAYTON SUPPLYING THE WORLD

WITH OVER

FIFTY THOUSAND DOZEN ANNUALLY

SHIRTS OF EVERY DESCRIPTION, PANTALOONS, OVERALLS, WORKING JACKETS, LINED DUCK COATS, Through

THE GEM SHIRT CO.

GRAND FINALE—

"DAYTONIA" Praising the Industry Which Introduces Her to the World.

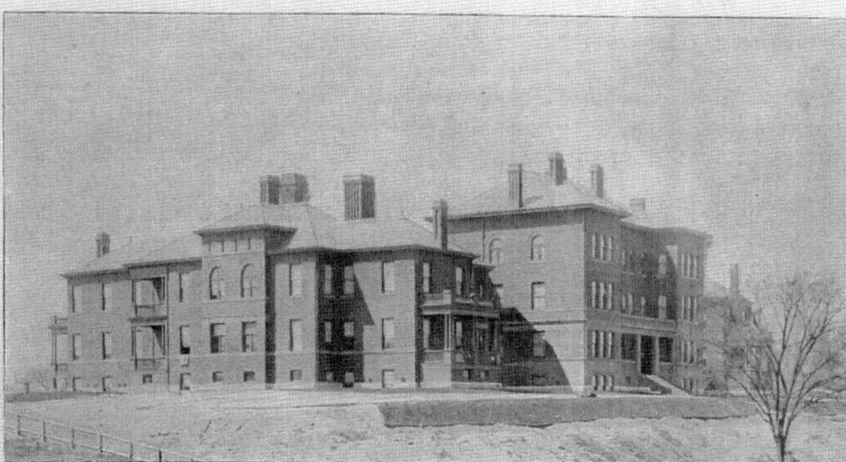

THE DEACONESS HOSPITAL.

This is no new form of Christian work, though the method and arrangement of this organization may be new to many. The term "deaconess" seems to have been applied in the apostolic churches to a woman devoted to special religious work. In modern times the movement which appropriated this name began in Germany in 1836, under Pastor Fliedner at Kaiserswerth, on the Rhine, where a hospital and training institution were opened, which have grown to large proportions. This movement grew out of a deeply-felt need for better trained nurses for hospitals, and also out of the conviction that Protestants had a duty to perform in relieving the wants of the suffering similar to that which had been done so effectively by Roman Catholic sisterhoods. The work was first introduced into this country in 1849.

The society in Dayton was organized in August, 1890. On the 18th of October, 1891, a temporary hospital, on Fourth Street near St. Clair, was opened under the direction of the society, and its usefulness proved that it met a felt need in the community.

The large, new building, which has been occupied since the 14th of October, 1894, is also a deaconess home and a school of training for them, founded and conducted upon an interdenominational basis.

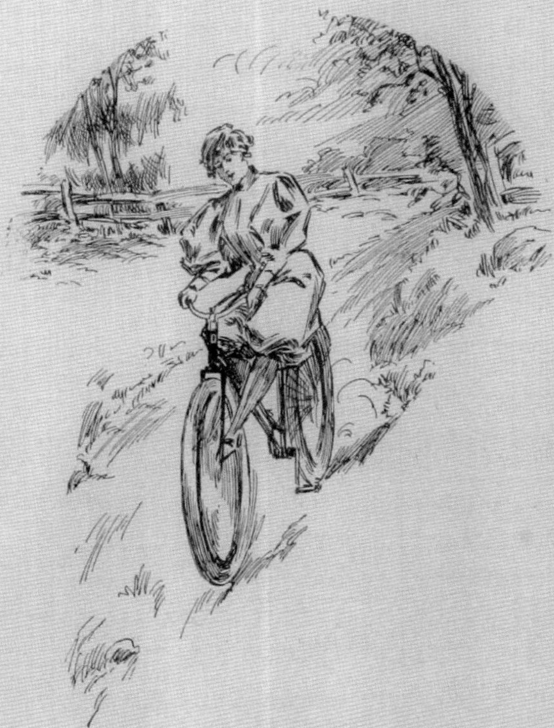

The
Crowning
Triumph
of
the
Century
is

THE

DAYTON BICYCLE

VIEWS ABOUT DAYTON.

COLONEL E. A. PARROTT.

THE broad, well-paved, and well-kept streets, the handsome grounds surrounding many beautiful homes, and the long rows of trees shading the sidewalks justify one in calling Dayton "the Gem City." But to appreciate fully her beauty one must look down and across the city from some of the surrounding heights. The framing sometimes lends an additional charm to the picture.

Our city is girdled by hills, through which, on the northeast and southwest, the river breaks a channel for itself and winds with loving embrace about the city on two sides. From the heights on the east, just where they begin to fall off towards Harries', there is a wide and beautiful view up the valley of the Mad River, and looking westward one gets a better idea of the extent of the city than from any other point with which I am familiar, since from this more of it lies open to the view.

Then from Belmont there is another pretty view, with water in the prospect, including the Miami below the bridge and Mad River above its mouth.

But the one I think the finest, perhaps because I have looked out upon it for so many years and become familiar with every feature of it, may be had from the Oakwood hills. From where I am sitting I see on the right the dome of the Asylum, lifting itself above the surrounding grove; in the foreground, on the shoulder of the hill, is Woodland, all the somber features of which just now are hidden away beneath the thick foliage of the trees. Farther out towards the northeast, across the factory chimneys, with their flags of smoke, the hills meet the eye again, seeming to rise in tiers to the sky line.

A grove of maples cuts off the view of the city directly in front of me, but a little to the left there is a break, through which one gets glimpses of bits of the river, and of bush-grown islets, and the river bridges, and Dayton View, climbing the terrace-like hills, and beyond, the woods meeting the horizon.

There is a misty look about these distant hills that reminds one of the cloudy atmosphere of the mountains — not the snow-capped peaks of Switzerland, but those that rise above the banks of "the blue Juniata," along which one rides on the Pennsylvania Central.

Directly to my left I look across a broad valley and see the sluggish canal and the Miami winding like a silver thread around the base of the hills, and on the rising grounds across the river broad farms, on the open spaces of which the floating clouds make pictures of light and shade; and then the Soldiers' Home, and the flag, for which so many of these old fellows gave health and limbs, floating to the breeze.

Space does not allow me to speak of the glories of our woods in autumn, when the elm and the maple and the sumac are all waving their gorgeous banners of yellow and crimson and red, nor of the charms which even winter lays upon the hillsides and the rivers, no longer hidden under the foliage of the skirting woods.

Beautiful, indeed, for situation is the city in which we dwell.

Cooper Insurance Co. OF DAYTON, OHIO.

W. P. CALLAHAN, President.
C. D. MEAD, Vice-President.
CHAS. W. SCHENK, Secretary.

Excelsior Bottling Works.

FACTORIES:
KLEE & COLEMAN, Indianapolis, Ind.
THE KLEE & COLEMAN CO., Louisville, Ky.

JOHN KLEE & SON,

Mineral Water,
Soda Water,
Ginger Ale.

Selzer Water, Champagne Cider, Orange Cider, all kinds of Carbonated Beverages. Portable fountains charged on short notice.

Office and Factory, Cor. First St. and Canal.
DAYTON, OHIO.

Bowersox makes the most **Artistic Photos** this side of New York. They are equal to the very best in the country. Special attention given to artistic lighting and posing. Visit our new studio,

133 South Main Street.

Bring in the Children.

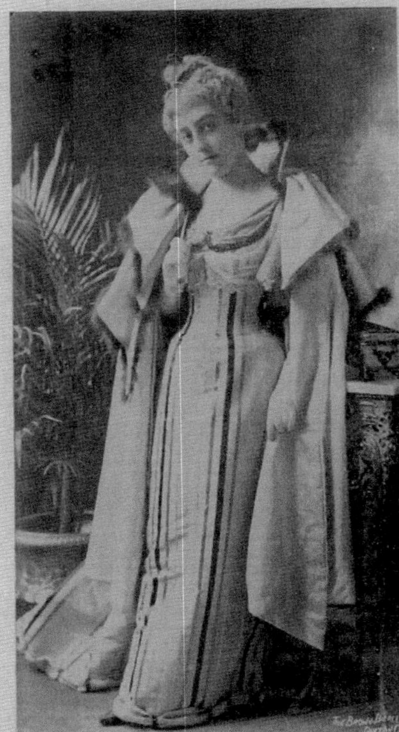

Columbia Insurance Co.,

Office, N. E. Corner Main and Second Sts., Second Floor Eaker Block, DAYTON, OHIO.

DIRECTORS:
E. M. THRESHER, ROBT. C. SCHENCK, O. I. GUNCKEL, E. J. BARNEY, ALBERT THRESHER, PAUL J. SORG, S. W. DAVIES.

JAMES G. STEELY & CO.,

DAYTON, OHIO. WHOLESALE **MILLINERY.**

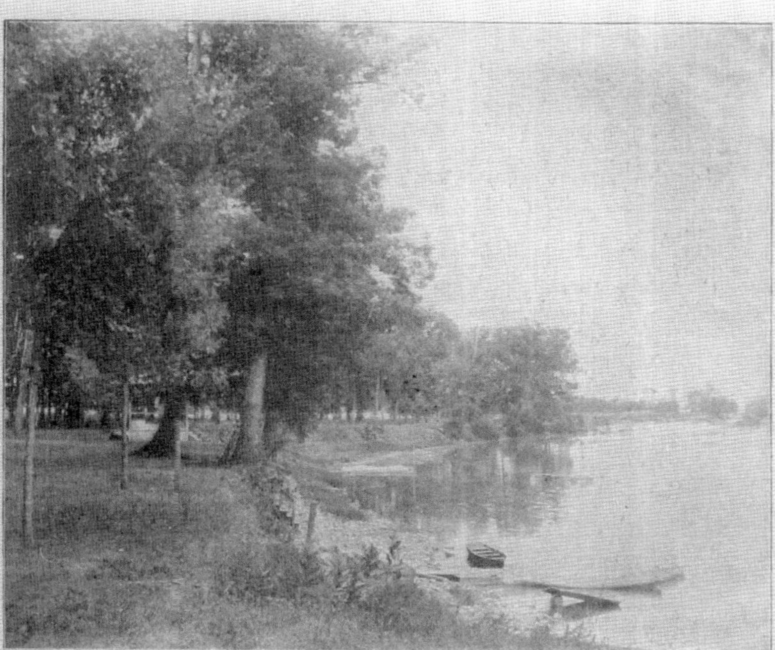

From "Early Dayton," by permission of the U. B. Publishing House.

IDYLWILD, ON THE MIAMI RIVER, NORTH OF DAYTON.

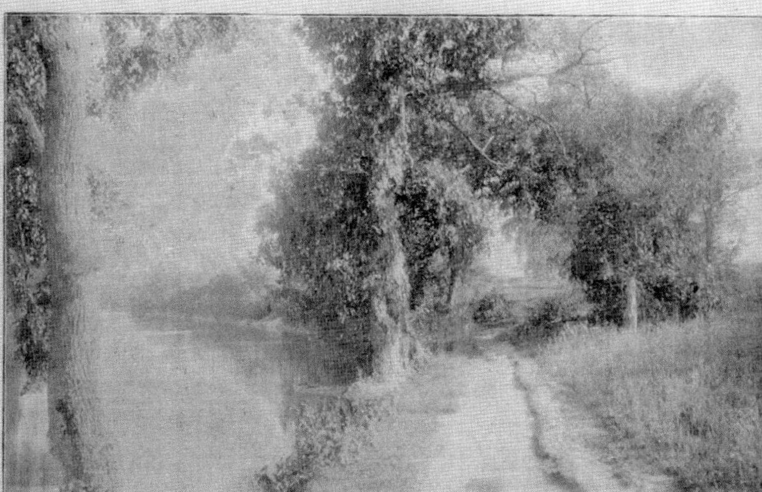

From "Early Dayton," by permission of the U. B. Publishing House.

A VIEW ON STILLWATER, NEAR ITS CONFLUENCE WITH THE MIAMI.

CHAS. E. PEASE, Prest. E. G. PEASE, V. Pres. W. B. ANDERSON, Secy.

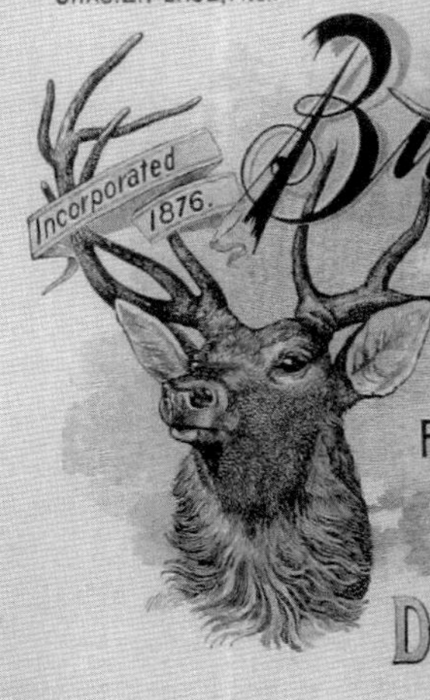

Incorporated 1876.

Buckeye Iron & Brass Works.

· Brass Goods ·

For Engine Builders, Steam & Water Fitters,

Tobacco Cutting Machinery,

Linseed & Cotton Seed Oil Machinery.

Dayton, Ohio. U.S.A.

CINCINNATI HAMILTON & DAYTON R.R. CH&D CINCINNATI INDIANAPOLIS CHICAGO DAYTON TOLEDO DETROIT

The

Pioneer Line of Dayton.

The Tourist Line to all

MICHIGAN and CANADA SUMMER RESORTS.

The Popular Line to

CHICAGO, ST. LOUIS, INDIANAPOLIS, and ALL POINTS WEST.

CINCINNATI and Points South and East.

MODERN EQUIPMENT AND BEST OF TRAIN SERVICE.

For Tickets to all Points and Full Information Apply at City Ticket Office,

No. 9 SOUTH MAIN STREET.

C. G. WALDO, *General Manager.*
D. G. EDWARDS, *Pass.-Traffic Manager.*

THE FLORA OF DAYTON.

PHILLIPS.

AN old book of paintings, by John W. Van Cleve. of the flowers native in this region is a valued possession in the household of one of those children of nearly fifty years ago, who learned the secrets of nature from his lips and the love of nature from his life. "The Beauties of Flora," as he called his little book, contains the most delicate of water-color sketches, not done in the impressionist style of to-day, but with a minuteness of detail which shows even the tiniest of veins, telling better than words the artist's careful study and love of flowers, and giving us, who have followed him, a delightful glimpse of what has been lost in the growth of our much-loved city.

Though many of the bright little blossoms which adorn the pages of this book are strange to us, yet there are many old friends. The spring beauty still peeps out of the grass in almost every bit of woods about us; we still find the frail little anemone and the sturdy bloodroot, both of which come and go so suddenly, and are so different in every other respect; now and then we meet the St. Jacob's ladder, with its delicate little blue bells; the wild sweet-william still scents the air, and along a little stream south of town one can see every spring the bright faces of the marsh marigolds; but the blue-eyed Mary, the "painted cup," and the Indian pipe, with many others which Mr. Van Cleve pictures by the side of our own favorites, are unknown to all of us not learned in the lore of flowers.

We are all familiar with the hepatica, and in marshy places the wild flag still grows, while shady spots by the riverside often shelter little clusters of Dutchmen's breeches; but how often do we meet the fringed gentian or a bit of spiderwort, the moccasin plant or the pride of Ohio? and even the trillium, that most pure and beautiful of our native flowers, is no longer easy to find. Every one knows how faithful the dear little violet is, but when I see how many varieties old John Van Cleve knew I come to the conclusion that our violet is the only kind that is "true blue."

Delicate and dainty as are our spring and early summer blooms, no pen can do justice to the wild roses, the goldenrod, and the asters that deck our fields late in the summer and fall, crowning the departing season with a glory which almost, if not quite, equals that which is bestowed by the frost upon the late months, when he turns the trees to crimson and gold.

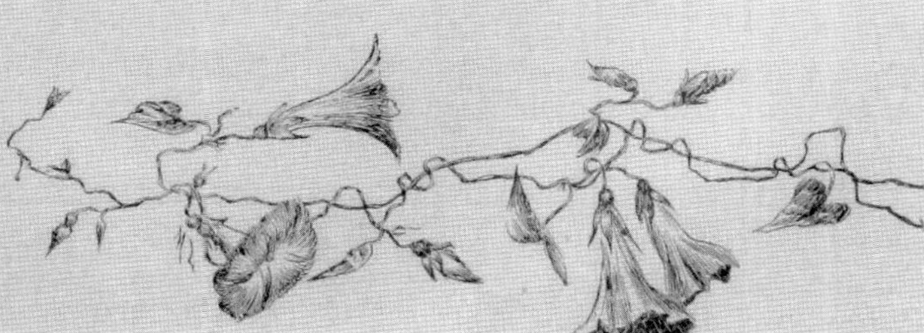

ESTABLISHED 1813. ORGANIZED 1865

Dayton National Bank,

WM. H. SIMMS, President.
S. W. DAVIES, Vice-President.
JAS. A. MARTIN, Cashier.

Dayton, Ohio.

S. E. COR. THIRD AND JEFFERSON.

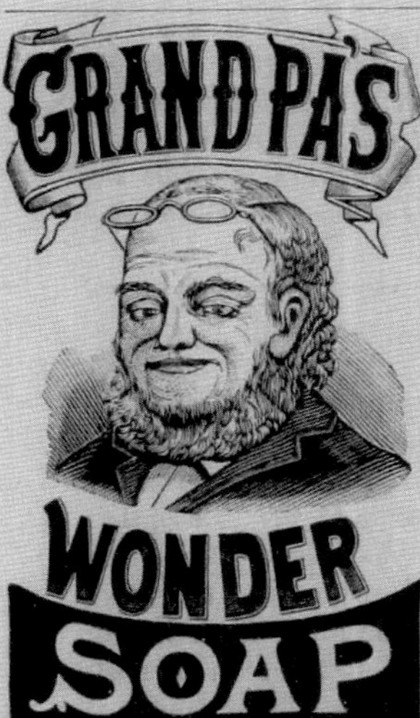

THE
BEST SOAP
MADE FOR
**Machinists,
Mechanics,
Engineers,
Firemen,
Foundrymen,
Miners,
Coal Handlers,
Printers,
Painters,
Farmers, &c., &c.**

Grandpa's Wonder Soap.

✻ ✻ ✻

Will make the skin soft.
Will cure Eczema.
Will cure chapped hands.
Will remove dandruff.
Will keep the hair from falling out.
Will remove tar or grease from silk or woolen fabrics.

ENGLE, KRAMER & CO.,

HARDWARE,

Dayton, Ohio.

LEGLER, BARLOW & CO.,

Importers and Jobbers . . . **Dry Goods and Notions,**

—MANUFACTURERS OF—

OVERALLS, SHIRTS, and DUCK COATS.

GRAND OPERA HOUSE

One Solid Week, Commencing Monday, May 18

Six Nights

DAYTONIA

By Mr. HARRY E. FEICHT

Grand Historical Spectacular, given by the Ladies and Gentlemen of Dayton to commemorate Dayton's Centennial Year. Proceeds to be equally divided between the St. Elizabeth and Deaconess Hospitals.

The Queen City Printing Ink Co.,

CINCINNATI, OHIO,

Furnished the Ink for This Program.

THE CORNS FENCE & FOUNDRY CO.,

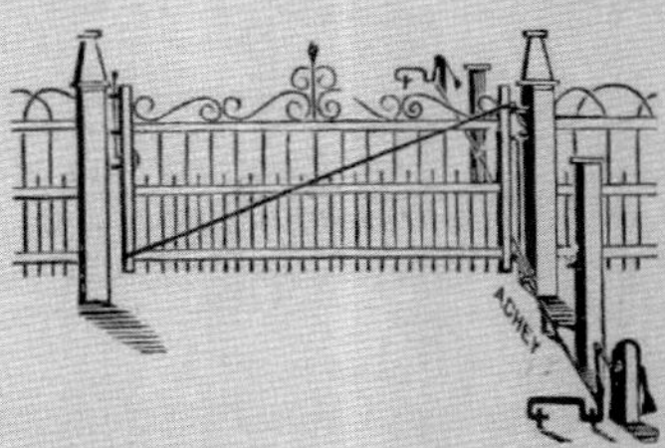

20 East Shawnee Street, DAYTON, OHIO.

THE AULL BROS.

PAPER & BOX CO.,

DAYTON, OHIO.

THE DAYTON STEAM BOILER CO.,

DAYTON, OHIO,

"THE ONLY BOILER MAKERS."

THE DURST MILLING CO.,

MANUFACTURERS OF

DURST'S BEST AND BLUE BELL FLOUR.

ASK YOUR GROCERS FOR IT.

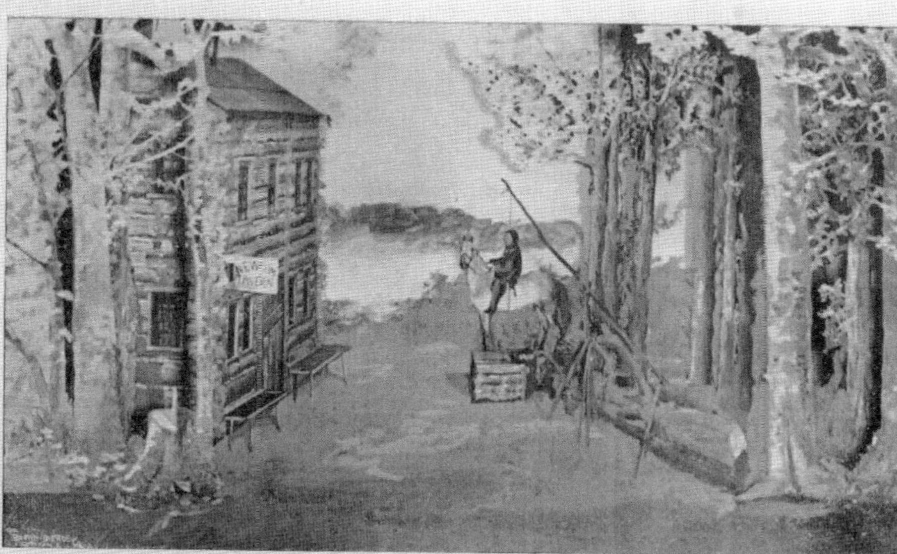

FLASH-LIGHT PHOTOGRAPH OF THE FIRST ACT OF DAYTONIA.

ACT I.

Will you see the players well bestowed? . . .
They are the abstracts and brief chronicles of the time.—
Shakespeare: Hamlet, Act II., Scene 2.

SYNOPSIS.

SCENE I.—Dayton, 1799, showing Newcom's Tavern, Miami and Mad rivers.—Settlers, etc.—Arrival of settlers' conestoga wagon drawn by four horses.—Attack by Indians; arrival of soldiers; skirmish.—Sunset; moonlight; darkness; soliloquy.—Vision with moving figures, showing the Steele High School, with trolley cars, bicycles, etc., passing. (New mechanical effect.)

DRAMATIS PERSONAE.

COLONEL NEWCOM, Keeper of Tavern........MR. HARRY R. DANIELS
ABRAHAM, a Pioneer........MR. EDWARD G. PEASE
JOHN DAVIS, a Mover........MR. HARRIE PEASE CLEGG
EAGLE EYE, Indian Chief........MR. CARL LOY
COLONEL WAITE, of Continental Army........MR. ROBERT C. MEAD
GEORGE EMMERSON, a Pioneer Miller........MR. JOSEPH W. MEAD
BLACK HAWK, a Friendly Indian........MR. FRED. T. DARST
DICK, Son of Pioneer........MR. CARLTON P. ROUSH
JOANNA, Daughter of Pioneer........MISS LOUISE HOWARD
MRS. CAROLINE THOMPSON, Wife of Pioneer........MISS MARY P. DAVIES
MOVER'S WIFE........MRS. FRED. T. DARST
ETHEL (three and one-half years old)........LITTLE FREDA LUELLA MCWILLIAMS
MRS. MARY ROLL (ninety-six years old, first white girl born in Dayton)........BY HERSELF
JESSE BOOHER........BY HIMSELF
SETTLERS, MOVERS, SOLDIERS, INDIANS, ETC.

ACT II.

Hail, bounteous May, that dost inspire
Mirth and youth, and warm desire!
—*Milton: Song on May morning.*

SYNOPSIS.

SCENE I.—Dayton in 1841. Third and Main streets, looking north.

ERASTUS JEFFERSON, Davies' Servant .... MR. DEWITT H. BELDEN

SCENE II.—May-day at Steele's Woods.

One hundred and fifty ladies and gentlemen, introducing the crowning of the May Queen; the May-pole dance; songs by double quartette; colonial minuet under the management of Mrs. E. Raven; Dan Tucker; Virginia reel, and the usual picnic finale—the May rain-storm. Everybody runs for shelter.

DOUBLE QUARTETTE.

Soprano.	*Alto.*
MRS. H H. BIMM.	MRS. HERBERT B. BROWN.
MRS. FRED C. WEAVER.	MISS MAUD REBER.

Tenor.	*Bass.*
MR. H. H. BIMM.	MR. HARRY L. MUNGER.
MR. FRANK A. PALMER.	MR. HARRY B. TURPIN.

ESTABLISHED 1866.

The Dayton Malleable Iron Co.,

DAYTON, OHIO,

MANUFACTURE ALL KINDS OF

MALLEABLE IRON CASTINGS

REFINED Air Furnace.

TO ORDER.

HIGH CLASS
MALLEABLE IRON
CASTINGS
FOR
RAILROADS,
CAR BUILDERS,
AGRICULTURAL
IMPLEMENTS,
AND
SPECIAL
WORK.

Send for
Catalogue.

CARRIAGE
HARDWARE
AND
ALL SIZES
SARVEN
FLANGES
AND
WARNER
HUB BANDS
IN
STOCK.

Felt and Iron } **Roofing.**

Paving { Cement and Asphalt.

The Dayton Asphalt Roofing and Paving Co.,

16 SOUTH CANAL STREET.

ACT III.

Cease to consult, the time for action calls,
War, horrid war, approaches to your walls.
—*Pope: Iliad.*

SYNOPSIS.

SCENE I.—Interior of a Dayton home in 1861; "Breaking Home Ties."—The opening of the Civil War.—Brave brothers (two Dayton boys) display unsullied patriotism.

SCENE II.—Street in Dayton in 1861. Third and Main streets, looking north.
MR. CHARLES W. TERRY, MR. WILL H. WEIFFENBACH, MR. LOUIS KASMIKSKY AND GEN. SHERMAN POTTEEF, as the Awkward Squad.

SCENE III.—Off to the War, showing the Dayton troops passing the old court-house. The most thrilling and realistic stage effect ever presented. Apparently 5,000 troops, including infantry, cavalry, artillery, numerous bands and drum corps, will pass in full review of the audience.—"Soldiers' Farewell."

DRAMATIS PERSONAE.

GEO. WILSON, } Twin Brothers who have enlisted in the 93d O.V.I. .... MR. CLEMENT A. HERCHELRODE
DAVE WILSON, } .... MR. HARVEY CONOVER

CAPTAIN KISSINGER........ MR. PERRY W. WEIDNER

MISS MARGUERITE WILSON........ MISS GRACE MIDDLETON

LITTLE ETHEL WILSON (three and one-half years old)........ LITTLE FREDA LUELLA MCWILLIAMS

MRS. WILSON........ MRS. BERNARD FROEHLICH

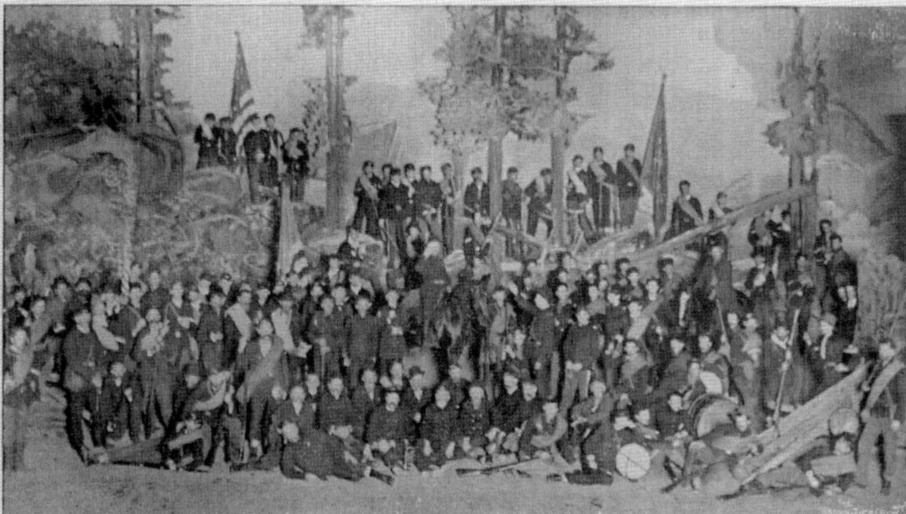

FLASH-LIGHT PHOTOGRAPH OF THE CHARACTERS IN "BATTLE OF CHICKAMAUGA," ACT IV., DAYTONIA.

ACT IV.

As we pledge the health of our general, who fares as rough as we;
What can daunt us, what can turn us, led to death by such as he?
—*Charles Kingsley: A March.*

SYNOPSIS.

SCENE I.—"Chickamauga at Sunset" (September, 1863), where hundreds of Dayton's heroes fought in defense of their country's flag. The portrayal of this sanguinary battle-field will surpass any similar setting ever given on the American stage. 450 soldiers will appear, introducing infantry and artillery battle maneuvers new to the stage.—The camp scene: songs and stories; moonlight; taps; on guard.—The Dayton boys' ride from Chattanooga to Chickamaugua; unusual display of exalted bravery; the hero's death; vision of mother; the unfinished task taken up by his brother.—The attack; the battle between the North and the South.—Lincoln.—Emancipation.—Peace.

DRAMATIS PERSONAE.

MAJOR-GENERAL J. B. THOMAS........ MR. ARTHUR L. RIEGER
PRIVATE GEORGE WILSON, Ninety-third, O. V. I........ MR. CLEMENT A. HERCHELRODE
SERGEANT DAVE WILSON, Fourth Ohio Cavalry........ MR. HARVEY CONOVER
ADJUTANT MORTON........ MR. THOMAS B. HERRMAN
SURGEON WEAVER........ DR. FRED C. WEAVER
CAPTAIN KISSINGER........ MR. PERRY W. WEIDNER
SERGEANT HEMPHILL........ MR. J. HOWARD DAVIES
PRIVATE MARSHALL........ MR. FRANK L. CLEAVER
PRIVATE HANLEY, with songs........ MR. E. W. HANLEY
PRIVATE BREENE, with songs........ MR. C. L. G. BREENE
JONES, THE COOK, with songs........ MR. DECOSTO
ABRAHAM LINCOLN........ MR. A. H. CALLAHAN
PICKANINNIES, UNION AND CONFEDERATE SOLDIERS... MEMBERS OF THE MILITIA COMMITTEE

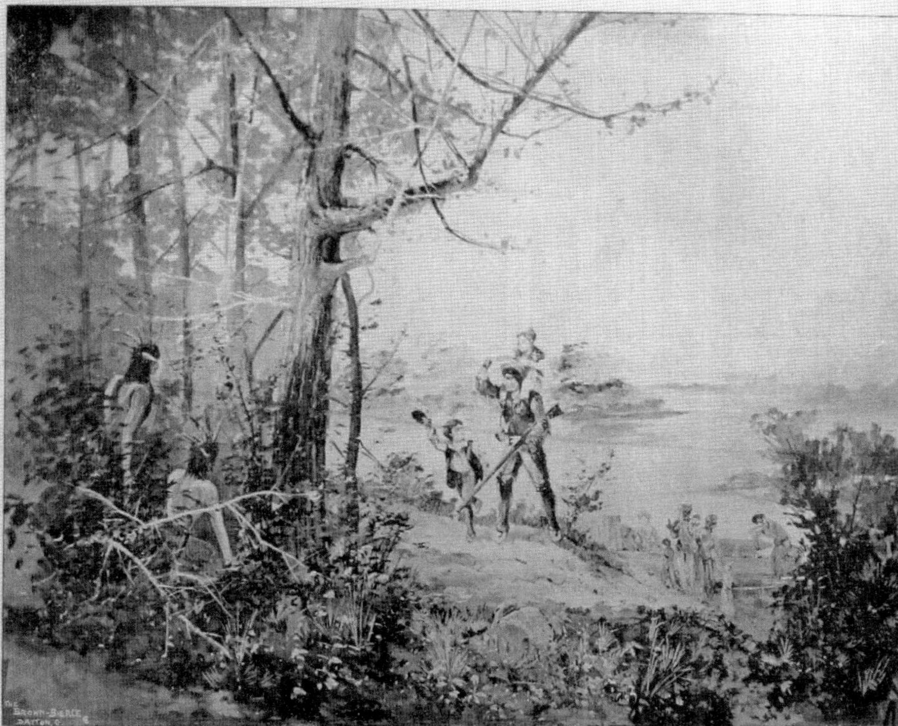

FLASH-LIGHT PHOTOGRAPH OF THE LANDING, APRIL 1, 1796.
First Transformation in Act V., DAYTONIA.

ACT V.

SYNOPSIS.

FOUR ALLEGORICAL TRANSFORMATIONS:—*First*, The landing, April 1, 1796.—*Second*, Dayton in 1829, showing the arrival of the first canal-boat from Cincinnati, January, 1829.—*Third*, Dayton in 1865; bird's-eye view of Dayton, painted from a sketch taken at Van Ausdal's residence, Dayton View, September 12, 1865.—*Fourth*, Dayton of to-day. Third and Main streets, looking north. The Gem City of America, ushered in by the Daytonia Guards, composed of the following Daytonians:

G

JOHN W. MARSHALL.
WILLIAM S. BROWN.
JOHN C. PATTERSON.
WILLIAM H. COLTON
HENRY J. CRUTCHFIELD.
DAVID C. HALE.
EDWARD H. MENTEL.
EDWARD MERKLE.
CHARLES THOMAS.
L. C. ADAMS.
JACOB J. SCHAFFER.

E

B. F. WENDLER.
CLARENCE G. WIGGIM.
GEORGE B. BUTTERWORTH.
J. W. GRANNIS.
JOHN L. BUVINGER.
WM. H. DRAKE.
HARRY H. HEATHMAN.
HARRY McENHEIMER.
EDWARD C. BECHTOLD.
ALBERT FREUDENBERGER.
CHARLES ZELLER.
GUSTAV A. MOEHLMANN.

M

JOHN F. KLINE.
G. W. SHROYER.
FRANK I. JOYCE.
U. GRANT SAIN.
WILLIAM MELKE.
WILMER W. McKINNEY.
A. W. ODELL.
ROBERT H. WILDASIN.
JAMES CLARK.
JACOB BERNHARD.
WILBER HEATHMAN.

The entire production under the personal direction of

MR. HARRY E. FEICHT,

Assisted by MR. JOHN W. WEIDNER, MR. PAUL KEENAN, and MR. T. N. WILSON.

Musical Director, MR. J. B. MEILER.
Special Scenery, painted by MR. FRED. E. KNIGHT.
Mechanical Effects, by MR CHAS. A. COMBS.
Properties, by MR. HARRY SMITH.
Character Make-Ups, by MR. PAUL KEENAN.

Mr. Feicht is indebted to Mrs. Eva Best for assistance in the first act.
The organ used in the production of Daytonia was kindly loaned by D. H. Baldwin & Co.

Magnificent Trains
of the

"BIG FOUR"

to

NEW YORK
BOSTON

ALL EASTERN CITIES

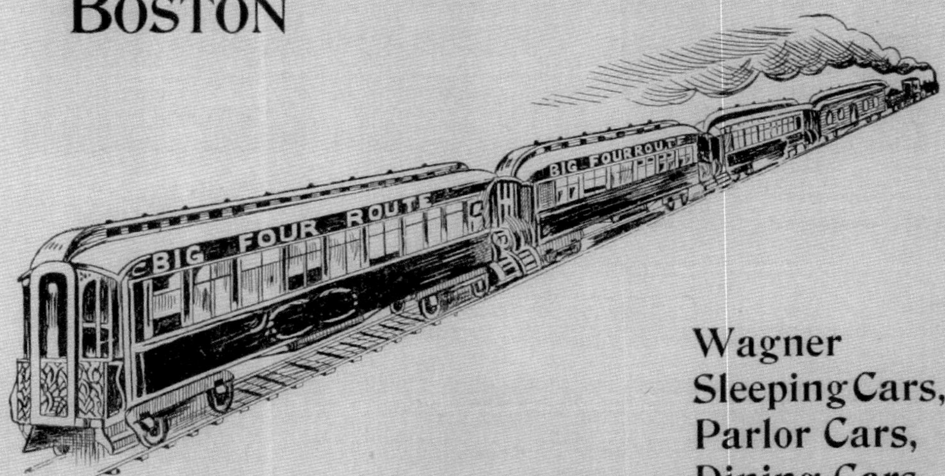

Wagner
Sleeping Cars,
Parlor Cars,
Dining Cars.

M. E. INGALLS,
President.

E. O. McCORMICK,
Passenger Traffic Manager.

D. B. MARTIN,
General Passenger and Ticket Agt.

JOHN L. MILLER,
Traveling Passenger Agent,
NO. 6 WEST THIRD STREET, DAYTON, OHIO.

COMMITTEES ON DAYTONIA.

Our praises are our wages.—*Shakespeare: Winter's Tale, Act I., Scene 2.*

EXECUTIVE COMMITTEE.

Director-General, - Mr. Harry E. Feicht.
Secretary, - - - Mr. J. W. Weidner.
Treasurer, - - - Mr. Chas. D. Mead.

Mr. J. W. Stoddard, *Chairman.*

Mr. Harry E. Feicht.
Mr. Joseph H. Crane.
Col. Charles G. Bickham.
Mr. Emil Reichert.
Mr. S. W. Davies.
Chief T. J. Farrell.
Mr. Harvey C. Phelps.
Mr. Edward F. Cooper.
Ex-Mayor C. G. McMillen.
Mr. Charles H. Simms.
Mr. Thos. A. Selz.
Mr. Isaac Pollack.
Dr. J. E. Lowes.
Judge Charles W. Dale.
Mr. L. V. Armstrong.
Mr. Paul Keenan.
Mr. Charles D. Mead.
Mr. A. H. Callahan.
Mr. M. J. Schwab.
Mr. Rufus L. Worrell.
Mr. Henry C. Lowe.
Mr. J. W. Stoddard.
Mr. Chas. J. Geyer.
Mr. J. W. Weidner.
Mr. R. P. Burkhardt.
Mr. Harry Weidner.
Chief Daniel C. Larkin.
Mr. P. A. McGowen.

Mrs. J. B. Thresher, *Chairman.*

Mrs. E. M. Wood, *Sec'y.*
Mrs. Joseph H. Crane.
Mrs. Max Wertheimer.
Mrs. F. J. Ach.
Mrs. Wm. Craighead.
Mrs. Eva Best.
Mrs. Philip J. Rottermann.
Mrs. C. J. Ferneding.
Mrs. Charles H. Ware.
Mrs. John H. Ohmer.
Mrs. Chas. H. Brown, *Treas.*
Mrs. C. E. Corpe.
Mrs. John Stengel.
Mrs. A. M. Williamson.
Mrs. J. D. Platt.
Mrs. Francis J. McCormick.
Mrs. Thos. A. Legler.
Mrs. Robert C. Schenck.
Mrs. Sol. Strauss.
Mrs. H. E. Talbott.

COMMITTEE ON LOAN EXHIBITION

Held in M. Ohmer's Sons' Building During the Week of Daytonia.

Mrs. T. J. Wood, *Chairman.*

Mrs. Chas. W. Gebhart, *Secretary and Treasurer.*

Mrs. Chas. U. Raymond.
Mrs. Wm. A. Phelps.
Mrs. J. W. Stoddard.
Mrs. J. P. Davies.
Mrs. Max Wertheimer.
Mrs. Chas. L. Koehnen.
Mrs. H. C. Graves.
Mrs. Jos. Klopfer.
Mrs. Robt. I. Cummin.
Mrs. John A. McMahon.
Mrs. John E. Gimperling.
Mrs. Susan H. Cammann.
Mrs. Jos. G. Crane.
Mrs. Martha O. Hawes.
Mrs. John H. Gorman.
Mrs. H. H. Weakley.
Miss Martha Perrine.
Miss Mary A. Gebhart.
Miss Fannie Dixon.
Miss Lizzie W. Hughes.
Miss Jacobs.
Miss Sophie Phillips.
Mrs. J. M. Phelps.

CONSTRUCTION COMMITTEE.

Mr. Joseph C. Peters, *Chairman.*

Mr. Jacob Oneth.
Mr. Rolla Gallaher.
Mr. Philip E. Gilbert.
Messrs. Kuntz and Johnson.
The John Rouzer Company.
The F. A. Requarth Company.
The Mathias Planing Mill Company.
The Peirce and Coleman Company.

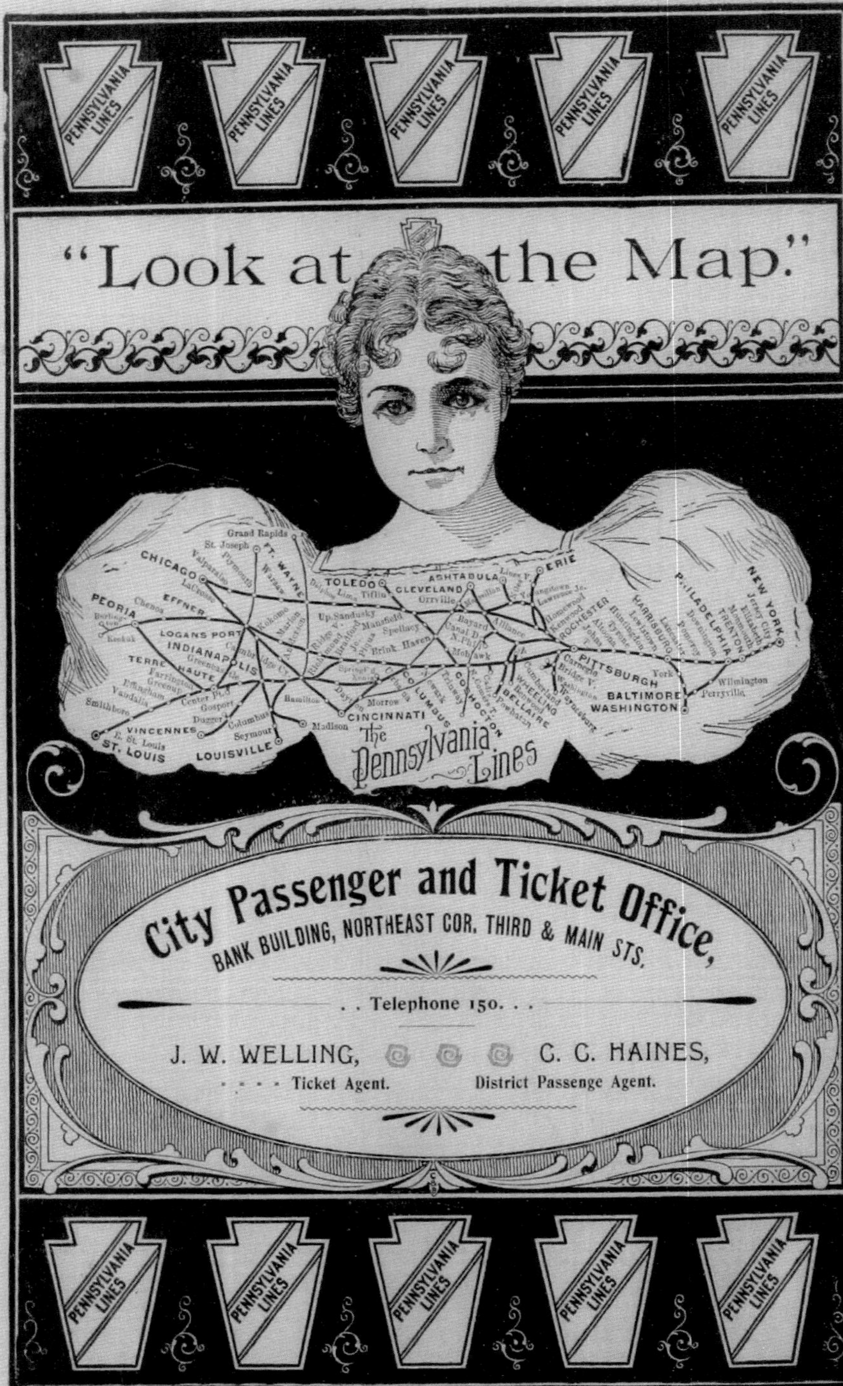
PENNSYLVANIA LINES
"Look at the Map."
CHICAGO
PEORIA
EFFNER
LOGANS PORT
FT. WAYNE
INDIANAPOLIS
TERRE HAUTE
VINCENNES
ST. LOUIS
LOUISVILLE
TOLEDO
CLEVELAND
ASHTABULA
ERIE
CINCINNATI
COLUMBUS
COSHOCTON
WHEELING
BELLAIRE
PITTSBURGH
ROCHESTER
HARRISBURG
PHILADELPHIA
TRENTON
NEW YORK
BALTIMORE
WASHINGTON
The Pennsylvania Lines
City Passenger and Ticket Office,
BANK BUILDING, NORTHEAST COR. THIRD & MAIN STS.
. . Telephone 150. . .
J. W. WELLING, Ticket Agent.
C. C. HAINES, District Passenge Agent.

COMMITTEES.—CONTINUED.

PRESS COMMITTEE

MR. CHARLES HARRIES SIMMS, *Chairman*.

Mr. Charles G. Reade, *Evening News*.
Mr. Abe S. Bickham, *Journal*.
Mr. Charles J. Geyer, *Herald*.
Mr. Harry H. McGrew, *Times*.
Mr. Edgar A. Morgan, *Press*.
Mr. Edward Neder, *Volks-Zeitung*.
Mr. John R. Tomlinson, *Journal*.
Mr. T. J. Wilson, *Evening News*.
Mr. Edward B. Grimes, *Herald*.
Mr. Daniel E. Kumler, *Times*.
Col. Charles G. Bickham, *Journal*.
Mr. Junia D. Uart, *Herald*.
Mr. Emil Reichert, *Volks-Zeitung*.
Mr. Harvey C. Phelps, *Sunday World*.
Mr. J. B. Siders, *Evening News*.
Mr. E. B. Brandenburg, *Journal*.
Mr. A. F. Thiele, *Evening News*.
Mr. L. V. Armstrong, *Press*.
Mr. J. C. Ochiltree, *Press*.

TICKET COMMITTEE.

JUDGE CHARLES W. DALE, *Chairman*.

Mr. John A. McGee.	Mr. Louis A. Pauley.
Mr. Charles F. Knecht.	Mr W. H. Shoemaker.
Mr. Joseph Schwab.	Mr Wood Patton.
Mr. John H. Swift.	Mr Chas. W. Bieser.
Mr. James A. Smith.	Mr W. E. Donson.
Mr. Albert L. Makley.	Mr George T. Wilson.
Mr. Will H. Tomlinson.	Mr. Geo. W. Martin.
Mr. Gabriel I. Pollack.	Mr. Edwin C. Baird.
Mr. Wm. R. Sullivan.	Mr. Albert J. Dwyer.

Mr. Edward G. Pease.

MILITARY COMMITTEE.

Captain J. A. Miller and Company G, O. N. G.
Captain B. F. Boyer and Company I, O. N. G.
Captain Mont. H. Bennett and Company of Earnshaw Rifles.
Captain John P. O'Connell and Hibernian Rifles.
Captain J. Philip Marquardt and fifty members of Old Guard Post.
Captain John C. Klinges and Commandery No. 115 Knights of St. John.

Daytonia Guards.

Captain John W. Marshall and Company **G** of the Blues.
Captain B. F. Wendler and Company **E** of the Yellows.
Captain John P. Kline and Company **M** of the Reds.

FINANCE COMMITTEE.

MR. WM. H. SIMMS, *Chairman*.

CAVALRY COMMITTEE.

MR. JOSEPH W. MEAD, *Chairman*.

Mr. Wm. H. McWilliams.	Chief T. J. Farrell.
Mr. John D. Geisler.	Major C. G. McMillen.
Mr. Wm. H. Crume.	Mr. Merrick F. McGowen.
Mr. Harry E. Randall.	Mr. J. McLain Smith, Jr.

Dr. Fred C. Weaver.

PICNIC COMMITTEE.

Mrs. William Craighead.	Mrs. Joseph H. Crane.
Mrs. W. F. Gebhart.	Mrs. John L. Brenner.

Miss Maud Reber.

Mr. Charles M. Wood.	Mr. R. B. Thresher.

Mr. H. C. Graves, Jr.

FLOWER AND REFRESHMENT COMMITTEE.

Mrs. S. H. Carr.	Mrs. Herman H. Ritter.
Mrs. A. M. Williamson.	Mrs. John Stengel.
Mrs. O. B. Brown.	Mrs. Philip J. Rottermann.

MAY-POLE COMMITTEE.

Mrs. J. D. Platt.	Mrs. Robert C. Schenck.

VIRGINIA REEL COMMITTEE.

Mrs. F. J. Ach.	Miss Henrietta Ach.

ADVERTISING COMMITTEE.

MR. MOSES WOLF, *Chairman*.

Mr. O. C. Schenck.	Mr. Adam Breene.

HORSE COMMITTEE.

MR. P. A. MCGOWEN, *Chairman*.

Chief Daniel C. Larkin.	Chief T. J. Farrell.
Mr. Maurice Costello.	Mr. Thos. Collins.

EARLY DAYTON

IS not a collection of reminiscences, but a well arranged and carefully written history of the city, from the social and personal standpoint. Its statements have been carefully verified, and the facts given have the best of authority. While it enlarges upon the pioneer period, previous to 1840, it gives a well arranged history of the city to the present time.

The illustrations surpass anything ever before shown in our local history. They include plans of the early city, the landing of the first settlers, the early log cabins, the streets at various times, prominent men and women of the city's early history, and fine views of modern Dayton. These alone would commend the book as one of permanent interest, as many of them have never before been published and cannot be found in any other form.

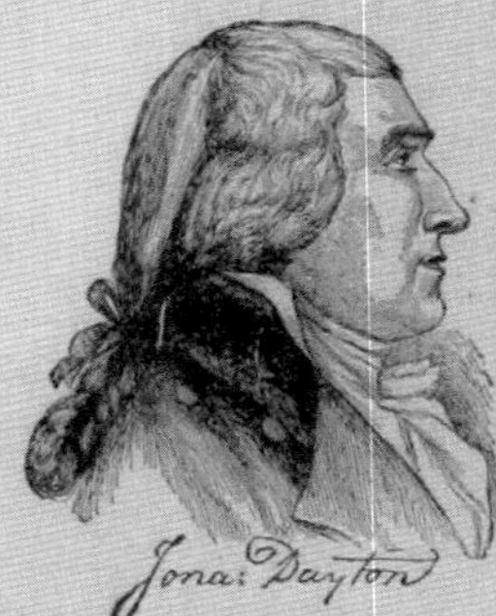

From the "National Cyclopedia of American Biography," by permission of James T. White & Co.

GENERAL JONATHAN DAYTON.

PUBLISHED BY U. B. PUBLISHING HOUSE.

SEE PAGE 28.

THE CRAWFORD McGREGOR & CANBY CO.,

MANUFACTURERS OF

LASTS.

ESTABLISHED 1829. INCORPORATED 1896.